Yesterda[...]

The Road to the Church at Disserth, Powys

YESTERDAY IN VILLAGE CHURCH AND CHURCHYARD

by

DONALD GREGORY

GOMER

Published by
Gomer Press
Llandysul, Dyfed
Wales

Printed by J. D. Lewis & Sons Ltd
Llandysul Dyfed, Wales

ISBN 0 86383 461 2

To my wife, Helen,
for her cheerful company

Acknowledgements

My wife took the photographs, except for
nos 13 and 21, which are reproduced by
kind permission of R. W. Soden, whose
copyright they are.
Part of the contents of Part II Chapter 6
''Games in the Churchyard'' appeared in
an article written by the author in January
1984 number of the Country Quest,
whose editor has kindly given permission
for their reuse.

Contents

List of Illustrations

Foreword

"And now it is all over" wrote J. A. Froude a century ago, "like an unsubstantial pageant faded. Only in the silent figures sleeping on their tombs and perhaps in the sound of the church bells can one hear the faint echo of a vanished world." It is the intention here to add some substance to the faded pageant, to do what may still be done to improve communications with the vanished world that once flourished so meaningfully within the walls of the churchyard. In that world everyone was involved in the affairs of the church because all tastes were catered for and all interests served, be they religious or secular, social or administrative. God and the devil competed there on equal terms; it was a matter of life and death. The majority believed in the existence of the devil and tended to see life as a stern struggle between the forces of good and evil, a struggle which was personified into rivalry between God and the devil.

In this study of the journey of the ordinary man there will be little need to talk of commemorative brasses, chantry chapels, canopied tombs and stained glass windows. Such treasures which provide much of the glory of old churches receive full and expert treatment from historians, whereas the object of this book is to put on record what may still be discovered about those too unimportant to have merited burial in the church or remembrance in a window or brass.

A note of urgency here needs to be sounded. With the widespread adoption of cremation churchyards today are far less in demand for burial than they were even a generation ago; moreover as the decline in the number of priests becomes ever more critical, many churchyards are becoming overgrown, especially in rural areas. In a remote part of Dyfed there is a round churchyard, almost impassable through brambles, which circles a little-used church from which life seems to have ebbed away, but which still has within its protective walls four sixth century inscribed stones. One priest often has the unenviable task of being responsible for five or six and occasionally even more parish churches, thus making the problem of seeing that churchyards are properly cared for a nearly insuperable one. In addition—and this is the saddest circumstances of all—there are now churches, some of which are of outstanding historical importance and architectural excellence which no priest at all can be found to serve. In such cases clearly nature will speedily take over the churchyards and the record of the past in another generation or so will be irreparably eroded.

The English parochial system was set up in Saxon times, the earliest parish priest probably being the chaplain of a Saxon lord, who appointed him and expected in return homage and service. Cox in *The Parish Churches of England* says "The actual initiation of most church buildings remains conjectural, though it may be assumed that the majority in Saxon and early Norman times at least served primarily as chapels for himself (the lord), his household and his dependants." The churches were built and paid for by local lords of the manor, but the priests, while owing their positions to the local lords, received their spiritual authority from the bishops, who were in charge of the various dioceses into which the country's ecclesiastical structure had been organised, under the supreme jurisdiction of the Archbishop of Canterbury. Nevertheless up to the end of the eleventh century, when new reforms came from Rome, the parish priest had to continue to pay homage to the local lord, swear fealty to him and pay an annual rent or perform in lieu some service of a feudal nature.

With the eventual establishment of a church organised on a parish basis, certain features at local level repay consideration, such as the shape of the churchyard, the positioning of the church within the churchyard, the actual alignment of the church and finally the building of the churchyard walls. Churchyards in early days were either circular or rectangular; the earlier ones were undoubtedly circular, probably in conscious imitation of prehistoric enclosures, which were sometimes used as burial places by early Christians. Hence it is that there are still a great many circular churchyards in Wales, even though many of the present churches may be less ancient than the sites they stand on, continuity of building churches on the same site being the customary practice; a contemporary guide to a church in Dyfed, which shall remain unnamed, suggests a different explanation for the shape of its churchyard. "It was made circular rather than square" it informs the visitor "so that there would be no hiding place in the corners for the Devil." Most of the early churchyards in England were rectangular in shape, a tendency that was reinforced when the Normans began building their churches, bringing with them the idea that was popular in France of "God's acre."

In many churchyards before the church was built, a cross already occupied a central place with graves grouped around it. The very presence of the cross more or less in the middle of the churchyard made it necessary for the church to be sited away from the middle, but even when there was no cross to influence the siting of the church, the church was very often built nearer the north wall of the churchyard than the south. A cogent reason often given for this is that it was not thought desirable for the shadow of the church to fall upon the graves. Another reasonable explanation is that, as burials had to take place in consecrated ground, the south side of the churchyard needed to be more extensive than the north side, which was unconsecrated so that it could be available for secular activities. The medieval limitation of consecrated areas may seem strange to modern Christians, who tend to think of both church and churchyard as equally consecrated throughout, whereas in earlier times only the place of burial and the chancel, where mass was celebrated, were deemed suitable for consecration.

In general, churches and churchyards were built north of the settlements they served; in consequence entrance was obtained through the south gate of the churchyard and the south door of the church. An advantage accruing from this arrangement was that worshippers would pass the graves on their way to service and were thereafter thought the more likely to remember to pray for the souls of the dead. Although this was the general pattern of building, with the entrance through consecrated ground on the south side, it was by no means a universal practice. When for reasons sometimes to do with the proximity of the church to the manor house, entrance was by the north gate and the north door, then the north side of the churchyard tended to be consecrated for burial.

Early churches in this country were always built on an East—West alignment, with the altar to the east, whereas the earliest churches in Europe had their altars and their sanctuaries pointing to the west. To understand this strange deviation from the normal alignment, recourse must be had to the advice given by Pope Gregory 1st to the missionaries, whom he sent early in the seventh century to follow up Augustine's mission to win back eastern Britain for Christianity. They were advised to be patient with the pagan practices of the natives, and, where expedient, even recommend them to accept some of their strange ways as long as no fundamental moral issue was compromised. Prechristian Britons had worshipped the sun and in consequence had built their temples facing the rising sun; hence they were allowed to continue to have their places of worship facing the east, when they agreed to Christian conversion.

The actual construction of the churchyard wall was regarded as a very serious matter; not only had proper care to be taken with the correct laying of the stones but what looks suspiciously like consulting the omens sometimes took place too. On one occasion a priest dared to make a comment within the hearing of the craftsman who was engaged in building his churchyard wall; the comment was construed as a veiled criticism of the lasting qualities of the wall. Back came the reply. ''Never fear; he'll stand right enow, for I built your shadow into him yesterday, when you wasn't looking.'' Sometimes the walls both of church and churchyard had deposited beneath them objects to ward off evil spirits, such as sprigs of mountain ash. Man takes no chances; he reinforces his braces with a belt!

Part I

1. EARLY BURIAL GROUNDS AS MEETING PLACES

No one today knows for certain the reasons which dictated the choice of burial sites in prehistoric times. Theories have been advanced but there is no clear proof. There are those who believe that Bronze Age man chose to bury his dead near underground sources of water. All this is surmise, reasonable or otherwise. Whatever the reason may have been, the sites acquired a great importance for early men, though it cannot be known whether this importance lay in some intrinsic merit of the place itself or whether it stemmed from the role it played in that society as a result of receiving the dead. In prehistoric times it is very likely that people foregathered for meetings in their burial places, which we call barrows, long or round, depending on their culture. Mortimer Wheeler has this to say. ''. . . it is likely enough that some of the stone circles were used for communal and secular no less than religious purposes in an age when the two were still essentially one and indivisible.'' That the long barrows of the New Stone Age were far more than just burial places Jacquetta Hawkins has no doubt. ''Their monuments must have served'' she wrote ''as religious meeting places, the scenes of the seasonal activities of a simple agricultural people . . . Their cultural association with the tombs was one much concerned with rebirth.'' In many early civilisations men believed that power in some mysterious way passed from the dead to the living. In northern Europe this idea is thought to be at least as old as the Bronze Age; in Scandinavia it was customary for a chief, when presiding over a meeting, to sit on a barrow, believing that in so doing he was likely to receive some spiritual inspiration from the spirit of the dead chief buried beneath him. There are references to such beliefs in Ireland, where popular assemblies sometimes took place in ancient burial grounds, while in England in Saxon times instances are recorded of hundred moots being held in former burial places. Indeed up to two hundred years ago covens of witches are known to have taken place on the sites of prehistoric barrows in the same hope that extra power might somehow be derived from the dead.

This custom of holding meetings in burial grounds, which was handed down from prehistoric times, was also observed in Wales, where the pattern of development in early Christian times followed a different course from that observed further east in England. From early in the sixth century AD Christian rites were being practised in specially enclosed spaces, set apart for religious purposes. Such enclosures which preceded the building of the first churches in Wales, were already regarded as hallowed places, partly by the presence of the dead buried there and partly because these sites had often been used for burial purposes in prehistoric days. The Welsh word llan only acquired its commonest contemporary meaning of church at a later date; in the sixth century AD the word was used to describe a clearing or an enclosure which had been set apart for religious purposes in a tribal community. It is perhaps not surprising that in these same enclosures Christian burials also took place, after all the area had already been sanctified by earlier burials. These burial grounds-cum-assembly-places were in many cases already enclosed by circular or oval banks. Such shapes were traditionally the shapes of prehistoric burial grounds, circular for Bronze Age burials, oval for those of the earlier New Stone Age, especially in Wales, where circular churchyards dating back to the sixth century are not at all uncommon.

Cox in ''THE PARISH CHURCHES OF ENGLAND'' said: ''. . . It must have been more than a coincidence that the first churches were constantly built in the proximity of prehistoric mounds.'' Certainly in the west many pre-Christian burial places were adopted by Christian priests and adapted by them for Christian usage just as many pagan and prehistoric wells were also sanctified and used for Christian purposes. Such is the conservatism of human beings, especially in the face of matters of outstanding importance like death, that, although Christians emphatically rejected the paganism of the past, they were quite prepared to maintain continuity of religious usage by burying their dead in prehistoric burial grounds, which necessarily were also pagan sites. Many instances could be cited of pagan monuments being made Christian by the incisions in later years of crosses on standing stones. In the Upper Usk valley in central Wales is a chambered long barrow in the forecourt of which are clearly visible crosses deeply cut in the stones. It is reasonable to think, though

impossible to prove, that these crosses were carved there in early Christian times to counteract any pagan potency still felt to be lingering there. This neolithic burial place bears the interesting name of Tŷ Illtyd, the House of Illtyd, an early Christian missionary and saint, who died in the middle of the sixth century AD.

For continuity of religious usage it would be difficult to find a better example than the churchyard at Old Radnor, in Powys. Originally a strong point in the Marches in the unsettled days that followed William's victory at Hastings, the hill town of Old Radnor came to be supplanted in about 1250 by New Radnor, which was built about five miles to the north-west of it. Today Old Radnor is little more than a church on a hill but it is a magnificent church, regarded as one of the finest in Wales, magnificent but only dating from the fourteenth century, because its Norman predecessor was burned down in one of the unending border forays. Old Radnor church, however, whether Norman or fourteenth century was built inside a prehistoric earthwork, whose flanks are still clearly to be seen on the north side of the church. The church, the churchyard and the prehistoric banks are all surrounded by a large circular wall of stone.

Further north in Powys, three and a half miles south of Rhayader and a quarter of a mile up a cul-de-sac off the A470 stands the village of Llanwrthwl, whose church is remarkable for its proximity to a prehistoric monument. There is a huge standing stone within a few feet of the south porch; it is hard to resist the conclusion that either Saint Gwrthwl, who is credited with having built the first church here, chose the site because it had been held sacred by much earlier people of another culture, or that earlier Christians still had chosen to bury their dead near the standing stone. In the latter event, Gwrthwl was continuing a religious association by building the church so near the stone. It is interesting to note that further evidence of the prehistoric past of the district may be seen in the Brecknock Museum in Brecon, where finds from Llanwrthwl include a gold armlet, thought to date from the late Bronze Age.

Another example of a church being built very close to a standing stone may be seen in the beautiful village of Maentwrog, in the Vale of Ffestiniog, as few miles inland from Harlech in North Wales. Indeed so celebrated was this standing stone that the village bears its name, Maentwrog meaning the stone of Twrog. Legends, of course, abound, which have lost nothing over the years, but the probable truth is that the stone marked a sacred site in the Bronze Age and that early Christians here, as at Llanwrthwl, chose to bury their dead in the same sanctified ground. The west end of today's church almost touches Twrog's stone, near which in the churchyard are a number of ancient yew trees, two of which, particularly massive specimens, are near enough to the stone to suggest that the stones and the yew trees together marked a prehistoric site.

The town of Corwen, also in North Wales, is on the A5, some ten miles west of Llangollen; its church, which contrary to usual practice lies to the south of the town, was, according to local tradition, first planned to be built on another site, but opinion seems to have veered to its present site because there was a great stone there which was even at that early time held in veneration. Today's visitor

may still see a stone built into the north porch; perhaps it would be more accurate to say that the church porch has been built round the stone which can now only be seen from the outside as the interior wall of the porch has been plastered over.

Still in Wales, in a remote valley under the Denbighshire Moors, is the village of Gwytherin, which figures prominently in Ellis Peters' medieval thriller A MORBID TASTE FOR BONES. This very ancient site of church and churchyard is bounded by a circular wall, between which and the north wall of the church are four standing stones, each about three feet high and spaced at regular intervals of about six feet. These stones at Gwytherin provide yet another example of the continuity of religious association, pagan and Christian. One of the stones is of outstanding interest as it carries a name which was probably inscribed at an early Christian burial, possibly as early as in the sixth century. The prehistoric stone—turned—Christian memorial commemorates one Vinnemaglus, son of Senemaglus. The church itself, alas now redundant, is sited on top of what looks like a round barrow and is surrounded by very large yew trees.

Another Welsh example, so unusual that it demands inclusion, is to be found under the western slopes of Plynlimon, just north of Devil's Bridge, in the churchyard of Ysbytty Cynfyn, whose church is so plain and unadorned that George Borrow, visiting it in 1854, when it was less than thirty years old, mistook it for a Methodist chapel! If the church is fairly modern, the site most certainly is not; the church stands in the middle of a Bronze Age burial chamber. Originally there was a circular earthwork with a number of standing stones set in the inner side of the bank. Today's churchyard wall is round; it contains five stones from the original Bronze age alignment, of which two, each about six feet high, have probably been moved to act as gate posts. Another pair seem still to be where they were built, while a fifth, a particularly splendid stone about ten feet high, is unlikely to have been moved. Nothing is known of the early Christian occupation of the site, although there was a hospice here in the twelfth century for pilgrims on their way to the Cistercian house at Strata Florida, twelve miles to the south of Devil's Bridge. All in all, Ysbytty Cynfin is an excellent example of continuity of religious usage.

Further south in Dyfed also there is considerable evidence of early Christian churches being built in prehistoric settlements. The churches at Llanfihangel-ar-arth, near Llandysul, at Meidrim and at Llanwinio, both north-west of Carmarthen, all sit on top of Bronze Age round barrows, while the south coast of what used to be called Pembrokeshire furnishes at least two more very interesting examples. Near Solva, high up on a cliff to the east of the village there once flourished a Christian church, which was built inside a prehistoric site; the latter has all but disappeared, while of the church all that now remains is the name, which is now attached to the farmhouse nearby, St. Elvis. Records survive in the County Record Office at Haverfordwest, however, from which it appears that the church, which certainly was in existence in 1291, was abandoned just over a hundred years ago, its font now being in use in St. Aidan's church down in Solva village.

Finally further evidence of the continuity of religious association comes from the very cradle of Christianity in Wales; south of St. David's, tradition has it that Nonna, the mother of David, gave birth to her illustrious son early in the sixth century at a spot where the ruined chapel of St. Non still stands. In the meadow that surrounds the chapel may still be found five or six standing stones, which in all probability originally constituted part of a Bronze Age Stone Circle.

East of Offa's Dyke the record becomes less clear of Christian building on prehistoric sites. However enough instances do occur to prompt the thought that many more may once have existed, though the different pattern of Christian development may well have made the using of pre-Christian burial grounds less likely away from the west. In Herefordshire, on the A466 between Hereford and Monmouth is the strangely-named village of St. Weonards, whose church was built fairly close to a tumulus. This Bronze Age barrow lies seventy yards SSW of the church; when excavated in 1855, it was fourteen feet high and a hundred and thirty feet in diameter. The church, like the barrow, stands on the very top of a hill.

In the newly named county of Avon, south of Bristol, at Norton Malreward there is a round barrow near the western entrance to the church, a barrow which is rendered even more conspicuous by the presence of a yew tree on its summit. In Dorset, at Knowlton, there is a ruined church which stands in a circular prehistoric bank. This bank is almost covered with yew trees; the prehistoric remains here are so considerable and so well-defined even now that clearly the church was deliberately erected in its midst to carry on a religious tradition, which had probably been preceded, as in Wales, by Christian burials.

Brief mention must also be made of the curious monolith that stands in the churchyard at Rudston, inland from Bridlington in North Yorkshire. Nearly thirty feet above the ground, it seems to be of glacial origin and it is thought that early man in prehistoric times erected it in its present position. Once again early Christians seemingly chose a site which to them already possessed sacred associations.

Finally W. G. HOSKINS in his FIELDWORK IN LOCAL HISTORY discusses a church which stands on a mound in Lincolnshire, called Maxey. He added this significant paragraph. "One suddenly realises that Maxey church may have been built here precisely because it was already a great burial mound, a hallowed site in prehistoric and perhaps in later times. Such a continuity of hallowed sites from non-Christian times into the Christian period is not unknown elsewhere. In Dorset the parish church of Moreton is built upon a conspicuous burial mound. Fimber church in Yorkshire is built upon a Bronze Age barrow . . . and Edlesborough in Buckinghamshire was built upon "Eadwulf's Barrow" from which it takes its name."

MAENTWROG AND LLANWRTHWL

In both photographs the proximity of the church to a standing stone is apparent . . . Early Christians, while deploring the paganism of those who lived before them, again and again chose to make use of sites previously used by prehistoric man.

In the case of Maentwrog (The Stone of Twrog) the stone was of sufficient local fame to give the village its name, though noone knows who Twrog was. In the churchyard there are many old yews near the stone, enhancing the likelihood that the site was of religious significance in very early times, thus encouraging early Christians to build their first church as close as possible to the famous stone.

A similar pattern seems likely for Llanwrthwl, in whose vicinity much evidence of Bronze Age activity has been found.

OLD RADNOR

Pictured here are the prehistoric earthworks inside
which Old Radnor's church was built. Men of the
Bronze Age lived here and, when early Christians
moved in, possibly as early as in the sixth or seventh
century, they once again chose a site, already made
use of in much earlier times, the circular churchyard
furnishing additional proof of this continuity of usage.
Inside the church the oldest object is a plain old font,
which bridged the gap between prehistoric and
historic times. In all likelihood it served as a font in
the first church on the site but it is even older than
that. Geologically it is an erratic boulder which early
men may well have used for some unknown purpose.
Such erratics were often grouped together into circles
in this neighbourhood in the Bronze Age, the best
example being the Four Stones between Kinnerton and
Walton, a mile or two from Old Radnor. This group of
stones, perhaps significantly, has a gap in its circle
where Old Radnor's font may once have stood.

YSBYTTY CYNFYN

In this photograph taken in the churchyard at Ysbytty
Cynfyn, near Devil's Bridge, one of the surviving
stones from a Bronze Age stone circle can be seen in
the circular churchyard wall. This particular stone,
the tallest of the five survivors, is probably still in its
original position.

ST. WEONARDS

No one knows the identity of the man who gave his name to the Herefordshire village and his patronage to the church. In the absence of fact fancy took over and identified him as a woodcutter and a hermit, who at death was buried in a golden coffin in a mound near the church. When this mound, illustrated here, was crudely opened up in 1855, the legend died because the diggers found instead of a golden coffin the cremated remains of two bodies.

Bronze Age man settled here on this hill-top because it offered protection from foe and flood; today the ancient church and the round barrow, close neighbours, suggest the pattern of early settlement here.

GWYTHERIN

The village of Gwytherin is situated in a remote
Denbighshire valley with high hills around. Its
church, dedicated to St. Winifred, who presided as
abbess in a convent here in the seventh century, is
now redundant but its churchyard, still well-tended,
presents a fascinating problem. Its situation on a hill
makes possible an earlier occupation by people of the
Bronze Age, a theory which seems to be confirmed by
the presence on the north side of the churchyard of
four stones, standing in line, each about three feet
high and at intervals of six feet. These stones may be
survivors of a Bronze Age stone circle. The problem
arises from the fact that there is a Latin inscription on
the most westerly of the stones. A possible solution
could be that the name of the sixth century Christian,
here remembered, Vinnemaglus, was inscribed upon a
Bronze Age stone; if this is the explanation, it
furnishes yet another instance of the continuity of
religious usage of an ancient site.

10

2. THE PARISH CHURCH AS A COMMUNITY CENTRE

Long before the Reformation the parish church was the focal point of the community. To the ordinary man what went on in church and churchyard mattered a very great deal, no matter whether it was in accordance with the wishes of the bishop or of the lord of the manor or of neither. The nave indeed was the parish hall, where the priest had little authority because it was not consecrated. In this meeting place many different kinds of activities went on on weekdays; business was regularly transacted there, announcements concerning which were frequently made from the pulpit, sometimes to the intense annoyance of the bishop. William Paston, whose letters throw an illuminating light on aspects of local life on a Norfolk manor, whenever he wanted to hold a manor court, ordered the priest not only to give prior notice of it from the pulpit but also to make it abundantly clear that every tenant was expected to be present. Many manor courts were actually held in the naves of churches.

Probably the two most outstanding features of the parish church in the middle ages were colour and noise. Pillars were often gaily painted and on the coloured walls pictures were superimposed. An entry in the churchwardens' accounts for 1597 at St. Michael's church, Chester states that the sum of one shilling and four pence was paid to one ''Robert Leech for writing stories upon the walls and laying colour upon the church door.'' As to noise, nothing could be more remote from the hushed calm met in churches today; an altercation in the porch will have been counterbalanced by a loud rehearsal of a play in the nave. Disputes about the ownership of cattle and land and suchlike matters were frequently dealt with in the nave, especially if the weather was too uncertain to allow an outdoor settlement to be made; in fine weather it was made on the north unconsecrated side of the churchyard. Again in the Paston letters it is reported that Agnes Paston and a fellow villager, who were in fierce contention over the building of a wall, which was thought by one party likely to hinder access to another property, agreed to meet in church after the evening service in an attempt to settle their differences. Apparently there was a very angry exchange of words, prompting a parishoner to attempt, as it turned out, in vain, to mediate. The parties withdrew to the churchyard, where, it is gathered, the two rivals went their separate ways, their quarrel unresolved.

Many churches in well-populated areas in the course of time had extra aisles built. This fact should not be construed as evidence of the need for more room for worshippers, but rather as an indication that more space was required for secular activities, associated with parish guilds and the like, whose functions, though entirely worthy, were more social than religious. In addition in many places the school was held in the tower, which normally was in the west end of the church; many an old church tower still shows signs of its educational past. If no benches remain as evidence, at least there is often a fire place to bear witness.

At the back of the nave, between the south door and the entrance to the tower, stood the font, as it still very often does; baptismal services were generally held on unconsecrated ground. Hence the fonts sometimes came in for maltreatment at the hands of the non-religious. In many churches it became necessary to have covers put on them and indeed in some churches fonts were kept under lock and key as occasionally the holy water was stolen and used for superstitious purposes such as curing sick cattle, as appears to have happened at Skenfrith, in Gwent; sometimes after a baptismal service the water used in the christening was secretly taken home by the child's parents and thrown on to the garden, preferably on to something green, like a bed of leeks. This was thought to bring luck.

One of the many ways in which life today differs from life in earlier times lies in the attitude of society to those who are ill or bereaved, visited by some sudden calamity or the victims of untoward circumstance. This century has seen the general acceptance of the notion that society through one or other of its agencies should make itself responsible for the unfortunate, whereas formerly the parish church sought almost single-handedly to alleviate the distress of the sick and the aged, of the poor and those buffeted by unexpected misfortune. Here once again the parish church stood out as the focal point of the local community, an insurance company and a welfare department rolled into one; surviving church records abundantly confirm the responsibilities accepted and discharged by the churches, for instance, in Cheshire, as elsewhere, the churchwardens, from whose accounts the facts that follow have been culled, made the decisions, which were put into effect by their officers, be they constables or overseers of the poor, who, like the

wardens themselves, will have been elected to office by members of the parish at the annual meeting of the Easter vestry.

Care for the sick is apparent from the following entries, the first four of which come from Malpas, a very large village in the south-west corner of the county. In 1660 2s. 6d. was paid ''to a poor woman who had leprosy all over her'' and in 1673 a boy ''with a scald head'' received 6d. Two years later 1s. was given to ''a poor child who had the King's evil,'' while in 1681 the entry reads ''Ann Mason having a sore leg 1s. (and later) 6d.'' At Church Minshull, north of Nantwich, in 1695 ''a man with his hand cut off'' received 2d., and in 1704 the wardens in Daresbury in north Cheshire, where a century and a half later Lewis Carroll's father held the living, awarded 6d. to ''a poor lame man.''

Evidence of help for those overtaken by sudden misfortune is also widespread; a few examples must suffice to show the general practice. At Wilmslow in 1612 12d. was given ''to a poor man of Knutsford'' whose smithy had been burned down, and the churchwardens at Tarporley in 1670 gave 4d. to a traveller who had lost everything in a fire. Two more quotations from the Malpas records deal with similar accidents. In 1673 a parishioner received 2s. 6d. ''to rebuilding the house that fell upon his wife and children suddenly in the night'' and in 1684 a widow whose house had been destroyed by fire was given 1s. and at Church Minshull ''three poor men who had their corn destroyed by the great hail storm'' received 2s. in compensation.

Miscellaneous awards covered a wide

variety of needs as the following extracts indicate. At Bunbury in 1672 Mrs. Allen "her husband being formerly a minister, but now melancholy and almost distracted" received 3s. Ten years later a "decayed gentleman" in Malpas was paid 2s. 6d. The Malpas churchwardens, moved with pity at the plight that had befallen Anne Yardley, provided a shroud and a coffin for her funeral, contributed a further 5s. towards the general funeral expenses, made an allowance of £1 and 3d towards the upkeep of two of her children and, in addition to awarding one of the girls 1s. 6d., provided her with a pair of shoes. The final entry in this section made contact with the world outside the parish, when the churchwardens of St. John the Baptist's church in Chester in 1723 gave 2s. to "a poor woman and her 5 children who were going to New England."

The church too had sometimes to act as the agent of central government; this enforced relationship had the effect of strengthening the ties that bound the church and the community it served. Cheshire's records will again provide evidence of this; statutes passed in the reigns of Henry VIII and Elizabeth I demanded the destruction of vermin, placing the onus for seeing this carried out on the already heavily-laden shoulders of churchwardens, who were authorised to make money payments to those in the parish who brought along the heads of vermin, which were on the proscribed list. Many different creatures in different parts of the country were regarded as vermin but society in general seems to have frowned most heavily on foxes, small birds of the sparrow and finch families, and, most unjustly of all, on

hedgehogs, which in some counties, including Cheshire, were known as urchins. In Great Budworth in 1665 the going rate for the head of a fox was one shilling; 2d. was paid for a hedgehog and a penny for a noup, a local word meant originally only to refer to bullfinches but which later came to include all sparrows and finches. Six years later in the same parish payments were made for 7 foxes, 32 noups and 283 hedgehogs; at the same time in Bunbury 253 hedgehogs were killed, though here only 1d. per head was paid. A century later in Wrenbury war seems to have been declared on small birds in general; in 1786, 708 dozen were killed, the following year 695 dozen, in 1788 295½ dozen and even as late as in 1843 bullfinches were fetching 3d. a dozen. Elsewhere in the Marches a similar picture emerges from a study of churchwardens' accounts.

One of the main activities that went on over the years in the nave of the church was eating and drinking; the church calendar had numerous special occasions which were marked by feasting and jollification. From very early times too patronal days were accompanied by eating and drinking which took place in the church or churchyard according to the weather. In the seventeenth and eighteenth centuries parliamentary candidates too were often proposed and seconded in the naves of parish churches.

In most parts up to at least the end of the seventeenth century there was a church house somewhere near the church, usually inside the churchyard. Few have survived intact and our knowledge of them today depends very largely on the repeated references to them in churchwardens' accounts. It would appear

13

that no-one actually lived in them, although the churchwardens spent much time there, doing the accounts and checking the stores kept inside. Certainly the ale was brewed there for the various goings-on and housekeepers were in charge of this operation. It seems very likely that in some areas after church ales had been eventually stopped, the church houses were let out to the housekeepers who had formerly brewed the ale there. Thereafter they sold their ale to the villagers and it is thought possible that some village inns that still bear names with religious connotations may have been the successors of these church houses when they became redundant. John Aubrey declared that every parish in the country had a church house, while at least in one Cornish village the church house was in use at fair times as a store place for the wares of itinerant pedlars. The day-to day maintenance of the church was the sole responsibility of the parish with the exception of the chancel which was the only part of the building that was consecrated in the middle ages and therefore looked after by the church authorities. Those overworked and generally undervalued officials, the churchwardens, had to find ways and means of providing for the upkeep of the tower, the porch and the nave. The commonest and most popular method of raising this money was the holding of church ales, which took place at fairly regular intervals in the church year, though the one held at Whitsun seems to have been the most profitable, possibly because the weather may have made it possible for the event to take place outdoors in the churchyard rather than in the more confined space of the nave.

The masters of ceremonies, the churchwardens begged as much malt as possible from the farmers in the parish, took it to the church house and there brewed as much strong ale as possible, which the parishioners would then be called upon to come and drink. The tariff seems to have varied from parish to parish but in some there were differential prices. The family man paid least, the bachelor was charged an average price while any stranger to the parish was made to pay for the privilege of being there. Furthermore good members of the community were expected to pay rather more than the minimum price. *Joseph Strutt* in *THE SPORTS AND PASTIMES OF THE PEOPLE OF ENGLAND (1800)* has this to say. ''By way of enticement to the populace the churchwardens brewed a certain portion of strong ale to be ready on the day appointed for the festival, which they sold to them: and most of the better sort, in addition to what they paid for the drink, contributed towards the collection.''

By the beginning of the sixteenth century church ales had run into a good deal of criticism. Henry VIII in an edict expressed the wish that there would be no more eating and drinking in churches; the royal wish fell on deaf ears. So far from dying out the custom seemed to spread because in addition to church ales bride ales were gaining in popularity in some districts. Here the guests were expected to pay generously for the ale which the bride's father gave and in so doing make a significant contribution to the bride's dowry. Again, in 1644 there was even funeral feasting in church when one, Margaret Atkinson, a Londoner left instructions in her will that on the

Sunday after the funeral ''there be provided two dozen of bread, a kilderkin of ale, two gammons of bacon . . . desiring all the parish as well rich as poor to take part thereof and a table to be set in the midst of the church with everything necessary thereto . . .''

In 1571 the church authorities had returned to the attack by trying to restrain churchwardens from holding banquets and public entertainments in churches but their success was limited, if *Philip Stubbes' ANATOMIE OF ABUSES (1595)* is to be believed. ''In certain towns'' he complained ''where drunken Bacchus bears sway against Christmas and Easter, Whit Sunday or some other time the churchwardens of every parish with the consent of the whole parish provide half a score or twenty quarter of malt . . . which malt being made into very strong ale is set to sale either in the church or in some other place assigned to that purpose . . . they bestow that money which is got thereby for repair of their churches, they buy books for the service, cups for the celebration of the sacraments . . . when this nectar of life, as they call it, is set abroach, well is he that can get the soonest to it, and spend the most at it; he is counted the godliest man of all the rest and most in God's favour, because it is spent upon the church forsooth . . .''

In the early years of the next century both protagonist and antagonist were busy. In 1603 Parliament forbade the holding of church ales either in church or churchyard, but with the publication of James Ist's Book of Sports in 1617 Whitsun ales were specifically mentioned as being permissible on Sundays, providing that there was no clash with the times of divine worship. The following year James I ordered all clergy to read the declaration from their pulpits but the order caused so much opposition that the king had to withdraw it. However his son, Charles I in 1633 once again ordered the clergy to read it and once again a great many refused; with the fall from power of Archbishop Laud the attempts to enforce the Book of Sports failed.

Nearly forty years later the ales still seem to have been in sufficient favour for one, Peter Mews to versify thus in 1671.

> ''The Churches much owe, as we all do knowe.
> For when they be drooping and ready to fail,
> By a Whitsun or church ale up again they shall go
> And owe their repairing to a pot of good ale.''

Three years later still there was another Whitsun ale at Brentford, for in 1674 the churchwardens' accounts there contain this reference. ''Paid to her that was lady at Whitsuntide by consent five shillings.'' Here and elsewhere it appears that sometimes a lord and lady were elected for the feast; at about the same time too clerk ales were still being held with the laudable purpose of providing the parish clerk with a salary. John Aubrey, writing in the middle of the seventeenth century about his own village in Wiltshire, said: ''There were no rates for the poor in my grandfather's day.'' In other words the church ales were still sufficiently popular to preclude the necessity of levying a poor rate.

Christina Hole in *A DICTIONARY OF BRITISH FOLK CUSTOMS* adds an interesting footnote. ''Woodstock's

Whitsun ale lasted longer than most of
the ales that once flourished in villages up
and down the country . . . at least in its
later days it seems to have lost its early
character as a practical money-raising
event for the parish needs and to have
become far more a boisterous festival . . .
the people danced and sang, ate, drank
and sometimes got drunk, set up their
summer bowers in the churchyard, played
games and loudly welcomed the Morris
dancers in their ribbons and bells . . . by
the nineteeenth century with only a few
exceptions the whole custom was gone
and was no more than a fading memory."

3.   THE ROLE OF THE CHURCHWARDEN

The key figure in the parish in the past
was always the churchwarden. The most
widespread arrangement was for two
churchwardens to be elected every Easter
at the vestry meeting; there were however
variations both in methods of selection
and in the number of wardens chosen.
Most parishes had two, the vicar's warden
and the people's, the latter elected by the
meeting of the parishioners, the former
either elected in the same way or
appointed by the priest. Sometimes
parishes had more than two wardens, in
which case the patrons or local
landowners made the extra appointments,
while just occasionally corporate bodies,
such as towns, exercised a time-honoured
right to appoint a churchwarden. At
Prestbury, in Cheshire, there were four
wardens, two for the people, and one each
for the priest and the patron. Whatever
their number and their method of
appointment, these wardens were
thereafter for their term of office
responsible for every activity in the
parish.

Here is the voluntary principle seen
triumphantly in action. Society in the
middle ages and indeed later was never
better served than by her churchwardens;
so multifarious were their duties, so vast
the field of their responsibilities that it
almost defies credibility that year after
year the Easter vestry meeting produced
new candidates for office. All the
corporate life of the local community was
in the care of the churchwarden to whom
very considerable powers were
successfully delegated. Of all the sources
readily available to students of local
history none is more rewarding than

churchwardens' accounts, of which happily there is a large quantity still surviving, to be found either in county record offices or even occasionally still in their original home, the parish chest at the back of the parish church or under the tower at the west end of the church.

At this same vestry meeting a parish constable was also elected, his main task being to carry out the instructions given him by the churchwardens; his duties included whipping and putting in the stocks those unfortunate parishoners referred to him for punishment by the wardens. Many misdemeanours, petty and otherwise, were punished in this way by the constable; the three commonest miscreants seem to have been vagrants, drunkards and scolds. In some parishes the whipping posts and the stocks were set up in the churchyard, from which position they were sometimes moved at a later date to a resting place inside the church, often under the tower, as at Llywel, in Powys, while in another church in the same area at Llanfryant the first occupant of the eighteenth century pair of stocks was the hapless carpenter who had made them, his offence being over-indulgence in alcohol, bought with the wages of his labour!

The annual parish meeting also elected two men, whose public duty involved representing the parish at the annual meeting of the synod, called by the bishop and the archdeacon, to consider the state of the various parishes in the area and the ways in which the parish priests were discharging their duties. These synodsmen, or sidesmen as they rapidly became, were required under oath to report at this synod on the behaviour of their priests. Armed with the sidesmen's report once a year the archdeacon descended upon the parish to make his own inspection before in turn reporting to the bishop. After the Reformation the duties of the sidesman were often amalgamated with those of the churchwardens.

Between them the churchwardens at one time or another became virtually responsible for every aspect of civil life at the local level; the raising and spending of money, the provision of relief for the poor, the sick, the needy and the orphans, the upholding of law and order, the punishment of all those who broke the laws of God as well as those of man, the organisation of public amusements, the maintenance of public buildings and the preservation of fences and boundaries.

The day to day maintenance of the church, the repainting of figures on the walls, (so essential in days when most people were unable to read) the keeping of the fabric in repair, these and other such things were normally paid for by money raised in church ales. Often however much heavier expenses had to be met, especially in the fourteenth and fifteenth centuries when many churches were either enlarged, shored up or rebuilt. Such extra unbudgeted-for expenditure was met by such money-raising devices as shrewd churchwardens thought fit to foist upon their community. It must in this connection be remembered that in these centuries man had a deeper sense of personal involvement in the business of living; this attitude precluded the existence of much of the criticism that would have been levelled against such money-raising methods in other ages. While every parish undoubtedly suffered from door-to-door collections ad nauseam, one of the most popular and acceptable means of raising extra money was the holding of archery contests. Wardens arranged them at the butts after Sunday mass, providing suitable prizes and as a rule collecting the entrance fees in person.

When impoverished young couples married, bride ales were often provided by the wardens and likewise bid ales were organised for the benefit of parishoners on whom misfortune had suddenly fallen. Occasionally if every other manner of fund-raising had proved insufficient, a warden levied a local rate, based on his own assessment. Such rates inevitably proved unpopular and are unlikely to have happened anywhere very often.

Our forebears made the most of public holidays. They certainly knew how to enjoy themselves but in so doing they were generous in their realisation that privileges had to be balanced by obligations. A good example of this can be seen in the annual celebration of Hock-tide, which also came under the aegis of the churchwardens. Hock-tide, the second Monday and Tuesday after Easter Sunday, was from the twelfth century a public holiday, Hock Tuesday being a rent day. The winter half-year for tenancies ran from Michaelmas to Hock-tide, the summer half from Hock to Michaelmas. On these two days the tradition of binding had grown up. On Monday young women, on Tuesday young men stopped members of the opposite sex on a highway and tied them up lightly with a rope until a small sum of money had been paid. The tolls thus provided made a welcome addition to the parish revenue and a wise churchwarden sometimes rewarded the energetic youth of both sexes with an extra village ale, which further helped to swell parish funds. This traditional ritual of binding came to an end early in the eighteenth century.

Parish life was for the most part self-contained, the community generally depending upon itself for all its activities. The master of all ceremonies was the churchwarden; he was after all the warden of the community centre. He arranged the bonfires to be lit to commemorate saints' days, he organised such festivities as the church allowed on May day and in such cases was responsible for the safe storage of the maypole for the rest of the year, while on Midsummer's Eve he was in the vanguard of the seasonal perambulation of the parish. At Rogationtide, early in May, when the Christian church had from early times attempted to offset the essential paganism of Mayday celebrations by arranging for ceremonies of their own, the churchwarden was very busy indeed, marshalling the procession, which, headed by the priest and the choir, beat out the bounds of the parish. Certainly this was a religious occasion but it was more than that because it was also an opportunity to re-establish parish boundaries and to clarify the ownership of land. At Rogationtide the churchwarden discharged religious, administrative and social functions, for the day always ended with a village feast, which he had to plan and for which he had to provide the victuals. When not actively concerned with the decoration of the church on such special occasions as Palm Sunday, Easter, Whitsun, Corpus Christi or Christmas, he may well have been trying to establish the paternity of an illegitimate child or running a vagrant out of the parish before he could become a charge on the public purse. In addition he had to act as a small-time banker and even pawnbroker, with articles pledged being deposited in the parish chest.

The churchwardens, as trustees for all the people in the administration of the finances of the parish, had to keep full accounts of everything; they had to arrange for the collection of all the rents that accrued from land and houses that had been left as bequests to the church. Once a year at the audit the churchwardens sat at the receipt of custom and all the men of the parish, marshalled according to their various occupations, came with their gifts. It was at this all-important meeting that the wardens officially took possession of property left to the parish in the previous year; here too they received from those with a surplus their contributions, which, as honest brokers, the churchwardens redistributed according to their wisdom to those they thought to be in greatest need. This annual audit was a great clearing house; most parishioners attended and the ordinary man received a very clear picture of how the parish was administered. He may well have felt the satisfaction of being himself a vital spoke in the village wheel.

There was an enormous variety in the types of gifts and bequests made to the parishes, almost all of which tended to be in kind. The large bequests were usually of land, whose rents thereafter became vital additional sources of annual parish revenue. Smaller gifts frequently mentioned included lumps of wax or even a swarm of bees, to provide wax for the church candles; candles were expensive and were used very sparingly. Most homes were normally lit only by rushlight, the precious candle being reserved for high days and holidays. Sometimes there were gifts of a cow, whose milk was to be given to the poor, or of items of clothing, thought suitable for being turned into church vestments.

Inside the church the churchwardens were expected always to be on the look out for those who broke the laws of God; theirs was the responsibility to report to the archdeacon's court all parishoners guilty of minor as well as major breaches of the moral code of the day. Very many offenders thus brought up were guilty of sexual offences for which the punishment was usually to do penance in the church porch, where they were made to stand in a white sheet. One of the best-known characters who was made to undergo this punishment was Thomas Parr, whose grave in Westminster Abbey proclaims the remarkable fact that he died in 1635 at the age of 152. In 1583, when he was reputed to be just 100 years old he fell foul of the churchwardens and in consequence was made to stand in a white sheet in his parish church at Alberbury in west Shropshire. The scene of this penance can no longer be visited as the porch was long ago demolished in the enlargement of the church. Thomas Parr's offence was that of fathering an illegitimate child. Officious churchwardens occasionally took it upon themselves to walk round the church during a service and, long wand in hand, tap on the head those thought to be giving less than their full attention to the service. It is perhaps as the guardians of the law that churchwardens received least respect; it is indeed difficult to uphold the law rigorously without becoming officious.

A random cross-section of examples of churchwardens' activity in the realm of law-keeping will show the difficulty of avoiding the charge of being officious. At one time in Yorkshire, near Sheffield, it was the custom during morning service for the churchwardens to leave the church after the second lesson, go round the inns in the neighbourhood to see that the citizens were behaving themselves, then return to the church in time for the sermon. Elsewhere in Yorkshire in the middle of the nineteenth century the wardens of one parish found themselves in serious trouble, when they were caught by the police drinking in a public house which they were officially visiting between the second lesson and the sermon, while in Manchester until the end of the eighteenth century the chief magistrate, accompanied by the churchwardens, used to leave the church after the first lesson and compel passers-by to come to church or pay a fine; apparently this frequently happened in some parts of Lancashire in the eighteenth century. Pride of place in this connection must surely go to the churchwardens of St. Peter's, Congleton, in Cheshire; on one of their normal Sunday morning inspections of the town they accosted near an inn a young woman, Ann Runcorn by name, who, resenting their cross-examination, gave them a piece of her mind. She was at once arrested and taken to a magistrate who ordered the bridle immediately to be put over the luckless young woman's head. Thus arrayed, she was led around the town, to be, it was hoped, an object lesson to all those who failed to recognise the full dignity of the churchwarden's office!

After the Reformation numerous extra duties were heaped upon the churchwardens' shoulders, though with the gradual breaking down of local isolation and the steady increase of central government, much of their earlier power faded away. Seventeenth and eighteenth century churchwardens' account books speak repeatedly of sums of money being given for the relief of soldiers maimed in the wars, for the provision of apprenticeships for orphans, for food and clothing for the poor and destitute and for the reward of bellringers for extra exertion shown on special occasions such as Guy Fawkes' Day. In addition they had the task of building pounds for straying cattle and setting up stocks and pillories. Suitable rewards for killing foxes varied considerably according to the discretion of individiual wardens, but unfortunately a great many churchwardens also rewarded, as has already been mentioned, those who provided evidence of having slaughtered small birds and hedgehogs.

Dogs as well as foxes, birds and hedgehogs figured frequently in churchwardens' account books; the friend of man was first discriminated against in the seventeenth century when Archbishop Laud introduced altar rails to keep dogs away from the altar. Thereafter dogs fought a losing battle even to be allowed to stay in church at all, although their champions seem to have put up a stout-hearted resistance! To cite but one instance, at Northope church, in Lincolnshire, up to about 1830, there was a small pew just inside the chancel arch, known as the Hall Dog Pew, where the dogs of the squire's family were kennelled during the service.

In the Marches too there was a dog problem. At Grappenhall, in north Cheshire, the vestry meeting was reported according to the surviving minutes to have taken the following decision. "We do order that the wardens of this parish shall cause the church during the time of divine service to be kept clear from all dogs and bitches by hiring a person to whip and drive them out of church." There and elsewhere in the county, and indeed throughout the Marches, churchwardens then appointed officers whose job it was to keep dogs out of church; those officials were also equipped with dog tongs to ensure the ejection of those animals who had escaped their earlier attention. From then on churchwardens' accounts frequently listed the amount paid to dog whippers, an amount which seems to have varied considerably in different parts of Cheshire. Only ten pence was paid at Prestbury, (admittedly to a boy) four shillings went to Edward Edwards in Shocklach, five shillings to Thomas Smith in Over and fourteen shillings, later in the eighteenth century, in Tattenhall. The job was upgraded, at least in Wrenbury, when in 1826 the title of dog-whipper was dropped in favour of beadle. Here in the previous century the dog whippers had been resplendent in blue gowns and yellow tippets, but in return for such magnificence they had a double duty to perform. For, in addition to dealing with wayward dogs they were empowered, thanks to a long wand, which they carried, to restore to full consciousness those who dozed during the sermon. At one end of the wand was a knob, with which they tapped men and boys on the head, at the other end was a fox's brush. With this it was thought more seemly that they should tickle the nostrils of offending females!

For a comprehensive portrait of a busy, conscientious and public-spirited churchwarden in the Marches, the reader is advised to turn to *THE HISTORY OF MYDDLE* by *Richard Gough*. Edited by David Hey and published by Penguin Books in 1981, this book deals with the affairs of a Shropshire village in the seventeenth century. Richard Gough (1635-1723) adopted a novel plan of writing a local history, recording the detailed family histories of the occupants of every pew in the parish church; in so doing he succeeded in drawing a marvellous picture of local life in Stuart England. In 1663, at the age of 28, he was elected churchwarden, a fact that is confirmed by the inscription on a bell in Myddle church. According to his editor, David Hey "Richard Gough . . . at the parish level helped with settlement cases, acted as churchwarden, drew up the glebe terrier upon the archdeacon's visitation and occasionally witnessed wills and appraised probate inventories." Rightly has W. G. Hoskins described the book as "one of the most entertaining ever written in English."

4.   TITHES AND THE PARISH PRIEST

Mention must here be made of the very real poverty experienced by many parish priests. Just as long as a priest had his living from his local lord, his financial position was assured but from the twelfth century onwards with the general increase in the number and importance of religious orders many livings were handed over by lords of the manor to the monasteries, which also received the complementary gifts of the tithes from the bishops. These livings were then redistributed by the monasteries to their nominees, who were known as their deputies or vicars. These new incumbents were rewarded for their labours as parish priests by the allocation of the minor tithes only, the major portion of the tithes going to swell the revenues of the monasteries. Other livings passed into the keeping of corporate bodies, such as the deans and chapters of cathedrals who, like the monasteries, appointed their deputies as vicars of the parishes. The salaries received by these vicars were invariably quite inadequate. These unhappy circumstances, which gave rise to a new type of parish priest, were a cause of great poverty and hardship, leading inevitably to the priests looking for ways and means of augmenting their miserable pittances.

Cultivating crops (and not just in the glebe), keeping pigeons, (there was a pigeon loft for forty birds above the chancel in the village church at Elkstone in Gloucestershire—and still there to be seen and marvelled at) and grazing cattle in the churchyard were all normal pursuits for poor parish priests. As early as in 1267 the Bishop of Worcester forbade the grazing of animals in any churchyard in his diocese. Despite such an edict, and there were many others up and down the country, the grazing of cattle was widespread. Here are three examples from the sixteenth century. In 1550 a vicar was fined for keeping sheep in the nave of the church, another was punished for grazing his horse in the churchyard, while in a third parish pigs were known to root up graves.

In 1671 the vicar of Woodchurch in Cheshire had to appear at the Archdeacon's court to answer the charge that he had pulled down the fence that separated the churchyard from his glebe land "so that his swine get in and roote up the graves." However, gradually opposition to cattle grazing seems to have died back with the result that parishoners began to take steps to protect their graves by planting them with willow bushes or bramble. The eighteenth century poet, John Gay, noted the ploy thus:—

> 'With wicker rods we fenc'd her Tomb around,
> To ward from Man and Beast the hallow'd ground
> Lest her new Grave the Parson's cattle raze,
> For both his Horse and cow the churchyard graze.''

Arthur Bryant in *THE AGE OF CHIVALRY* cites an example in a Devonshire church where a complaint was lodged with the archdeacon about the stabling of the vicar's animals in the churchyard "whereby it is evilly trodden down and foully defiled." The same priest seems to have made his malt and stored his corn in the nave of the church. As late as in the eighteenth century some parish priests, not satisfied with cultivating the glebeland, as was their right, were still growing crops in the churchyard. On one occasion the priest was reproved by the archdeacon on his annual visitation with these words. "Let me not see turnips, when I come next year"; to which the unrepentant priest, who knew something about a proper rotation of crops, replied. "Certainly not; it will be barley next time!"

One of the greatest causes of bad feeling between priests and parishoners from Anglo-Saxon times onwards concerned the system of tithes. In theory tithes amounted to a tenth part of the annual proceeds of the land and labour in the parish; this tax on income, for it was none other, was usually paid in kind and was stored, where feasible, in the parish barn. The tenth sucking pig however will have often gone straight from the farm to the priest's table! Tithe barns that still exist today are as a rule altogether more splendid than were the early barns in which the village tithes were stored. Such barns as the wonderful "wooden cathedral" at Great Coxwell in Oxfordshire belonged to monasteries.

G. G. Coulton, in *MEDIEVAL PANORAMA*, expressed the opinion that the tithes, which formed the greater part of the priest's income, added up to about a ten per cent income tax on the gross income of every parishoner except where, in Coulton's felicitous phrase, "custom softened the strictness of the law." G. M. Trevelyan quotes a country song, which was sung lustily every harvest time, as the providers of tithes renewed their annual resolve to stave off the worst! "We've cheated the parson, we'll cheat him again. For why should the vicar have one in ten?" The non-payment of tithes

had indeed been a sore point with priests for centuries; in the fourteenth century Chaucer, ever the friend of the under-dog, marked out for a special word of praise the priest who took pity on the parishoner who was late with his payment of tithe; instead of excommunicating him he gave him more time in which to pay.

Changes in the tithe arrangements took a very long time to come; there was certainly plenty of opposition but it lacked the means of finding a practical way in which to bring about this considerable political change. In 1647 at Tattenhall, under the Peckforton Hills in Cheshire, four parishioners were reported by their vicar to the local justices for refusing to pay their tithes. Moreover they were also charged with actively encouraging others to do the same. They were duly arrested and kept in custody for three weeks, pending the hearing of their case. What might have become a splendid gesture of defiance against authority that might well have started a public outcry against the payment of tithes ended in anti-climax as their spirit appears to have been broken by their imprisonment. On their release the four men timidly agreed in future to pay their tithes.

With the coming of the nineteenth century and the gradual piecemeal extension of the franchise to those who were previously under-privileged, change would become inevitable. Until Parliament however was forced to widen the franchise, the only course open to the opponents of the existing arrangements for paying tithes in kind, was by having recourse to the law court, a slow and expensive business. The Marches provide an excellent example of how such action was taken; in a remote corner of south-west Herefordshire, under the very shadow of the Black Mountains, which separate England and Wales, is the ancient settlement of Clodock, astride the river Monnow. At the west end of a large Norman church is an eighteenth century gallery, under which is recounted on the north wall a court action brought in 1805 by four local farmers against the vicar of Clodock. In an action in a civil court which took three years to come to a decision, six suggestions were made by the plaintiffs, namely that the owner of every house and garden in the parish should in future pay 6d a year instead of contributing fruit and herbs, 2d for every day previously spent in the hay field, 2½d. instead of handing over a cow in milk, 2d. instead of a barren cow, 4d. for every colt, and 2d. instead of a collection of eggs. The Brecon lawyer who represented the farmers finally obtained a verdict in their favour on May 19th 1808; thus in at least one parish in the Marches tithes in kind came to an abrupt halt. Parliament made the change general in 1836, when the Tithe Commutation Act passed into law, making an end to the payment of tithes in kind. This new arrangement was to last for another fifty years.

Kilvert, when vicar of Bredwardine, in Herefordshire, noted in his diary on 5th February 1878:—"Today was the tithe audit held at the vicarage. About fifty tithe payers came, most of them very small holders, some paying as little as ninepence. As soon as they had paid their tithe to Mr. Haywood (the churchwarden) in the front hall, they retired into the back hall and regaled themselves with bread, cheese and beer, some of them eating and drinking the value of the tithe they had paid." Had Kilvert but lived another thirteen years he would have seen the end of this annual charade, for in 1891 Parliament made tithes in future payable by landowners only. The last chapter in this long story of tithes, which began in Anglo-Saxon England, was written in 1936, when with the passage of the Final Tithe Commutation Act the payment of all tithes ended altogether.

BREDWARDINE

In this view of St. Andrews church the path may be
seen which leads to what was Kilvert's vicarage, along
which the fifty tithe payers passed on their way to the
annual tithe audit, after which, according to the
diarist, some of them, invited into the back hall of the
vicarage for refreshments, proceeded to eat and drink
the value of the tithes they had paid!

The Kilvert Society has seen to it that their hero is
fittingly remembered; there is a memorial seat under a
yew near the gate and his photograph hangs on the
north wall of the church. His grave is on the north
side of the churchyard, while the older, south side is
very rich in an assortment of table tombs.

Part II

1. THE CHURCH PORCH

As an entrance to a church many an old porch will seem quite out of proportion, if viewed solely as giving access to the building. The very size of many of these porches however will give some idea of their importance. Not only was the porch the funnel into which all passed on their way to the community centre but; in addition, it was a meeting place in its own right. The variety of the activities that went on there was even greater than in the nave itself so that it was almost as significant a focal point in the life of the parish as was the church itself. All porches had benches, some running along both sides and many had also an altar, a niche, a piscina or a stoup.

The original purpose of the porch, which was as a rule built later than the main body of the church, was to provide shelter for parishioners and to protect the church door from the weather. This architectural afterthought has had over the centuries the beneficent effect of ensuring for posterity many original features of south doors, which otherwise time and the elements would surely have destroyed. Many a splendid tympanum over a Norman doorway has in consequence been enabled to survive, of which two outstanding examples both in the Marches will be cited.

The church at Llanbadarn Fawr, a mile and a half west of Pen-y-bont and north of Llandrindod Wells in Powys, was virtually rebuilt in 1878, except for the south doorway above which may be seen in an excellent state of preservation one of only two surviving Norman tympana in the whole of Wales. The carving is believed to have been the work of one of the craftsmen of the much-famed Herefordshire school whose peak of achievement was reached at Kilpeck; these craftsmen were also responsible for the other tympanum cited, which is to be found further south at Rowlstone in the south-west corner of the Golden Valley in Herefordshire just east of Offa's Dyke. Here the motif is Christ in Majesty and it has, thanks to the protection afforded by the porch, magnificently stood the test of time. Sundials above the church door have too sometimes managed to survive thanks to the later building of a church porch, as at Kirkdale in north Yorkshire, where in the gloom of the south porch above the church door a Saxon sundial, now nearly nine hundred and fifty years old, belies its age, though of course once the porch had been built over it it had ceased to play its proper part.

Once the porch was added to the building, be it on the south side, the north or on the west, as occasionally happened, other possibilities for its use other than the provision of shelter and protection were quickly realised. From the twelfth to the fifteenth centuries in some places an upper chamber was added above the porch, which may well have become a general purpose room. Certainly some of them had fireplaces and many of them had considerable storage facilities. It is thought that in a few fortunate churches these rooms may even have housed libraries; probably the parish supply of arms was occasionally stored there too. Instances are known in addition where a night watchman was installed. The largest and probably the finest superstructure of this sort is at Cirencester, where there is a three-storeyed building, which was originally put up by the Black Canons as an administrative complex for the use of the nearby but now vanished Augustinian Priory; later the upper floor provided the trade guilds with suitable headquarters before serving for some years as Cirencester's town hall. A few miles to the east of Cirencester another excellent three-storeyed porch may be seen at Burford, whose churchyard, like so many others in the Cotswolds contains a great many grave stones of outstanding quality.

In the Marches there are a number of two-storeyed porches, Cheshire in the north possessing four architecturally outstanding examples, at Astbury, (where there is also a three-storeyed one) Malpas, Nantwich and at Over. There are in addition ordinary, solid, useful and unexciting two-tiered porches further south at Guilsfield, in Powys, and at Clun, in south Shropshire, which justify further description because this type of porch was far more common than the visually more exciting ones mentioned above.

Guilsfield, which lies two miles north of Welshpool and about fifteen miles west of Shrewsbury, is a spacious, civilised village with a history which stretches back to the fifth century when there was a very early Christian settlement there. Today's church, mostly built in the fourteenth century, stands in a circular churchyard, which is completely ringed round with yew trees. The large double-storeyed porch is square; against its west wall runs a sturdy stone bench, whilst against the opposite wall stands a large iron-bound oaken chest, hewn out of a solid tree trunk. Above the chest on the inner wall, just east of the door, is a stoup. The huge oak door, which leads from the porch into the nave, is four inches thick and still bears its ancient fleur-de-lys patterned hinges. Access to the upper room is gained by a staircase just inside the porch on the east wall; originally it was the priest's room but later for many years it provided the village with a school room. Adjoining the exterior west wall of the porch is a single-storey hearse house, which carries the names of the churchwardens for the year in which it was built, 1739.

Clun, where there is also a double-storeyed porch, is a small town of some substance. At one end of the town lies the ruins of a Norman castle, at the other across a narrow medieval bridge spanning the river Clun, is a Norman church, dedicated to St. George, perhaps a surprising dedication to find in a church so close to the frontier with Wales. The church is capped by a pyramidal tower, which is a common feature of old churches in this part of the Marches. Much of this very large church is still obviously Norman, despite the damage inflicted on it by war in the seventeenth century and restoration in the nineteenth. The porch, which unusually is on the north side of the church, was built in the fourteenth century and measures thirteen feet in length and eleven feet in breadth, having stone seats running along both sides. The upper room, now a store room, was, as at

Guilsfield, built for the use of the priest, but later called into service as a school. Access to this room today is up a staircase sited inside the church but vestigial traces of the original staircase may still just be seen in the east wall of the porch, on both walls of which will also be seen Benefaction Boards, detailing bequests made in the eighteenth century when, in the absence of any state concern for the redress of poverty, generous men and women, when they died, remembered to make provision for the poor and unprivileged of their parish.

In the middle ages banns of marriage were called in the porch, to be followed, where there was no let or hindrance, by the actual drawing-up of a marriage contract, which will later have been sworn before the altar in the porch by the parties interested. Before the Reformation the first part of the marriage service was also celebrated there; this ceremeony included the putting-on of the wedding ring, which had to precede the actual celebration of the wedding mass in the chancel. Chaucer bore witness to this tradition in his Prologue, where he introduced the Good Wife of Bath thus:—

"Housbones at chirche dore she hadde fyve"

Edward VI, in the middle of the sixteenth century, put an end to this part of the marriage service taking place in the church porch, the same monarch requiring women after childbirth to be allowed into the chancel for churching whereas throughout the middle ages they had been debarred from entering the church proper until churched in the porch. The first part of the baptism service likewise was at one time held in the porch, before the child and its parents were escorted to the font.

Many churches in the middle ages had stoups or piscinas on the east wall of the porch near the inner door; if the porch also contained an altar, a piscina would have been essential in order that the presiding priest might wash his hands before officiating and wash the holy vessels after use. Most of the recessed stone basins that have survived, however, are stoups which would have held holy water into which churchgoers would have dipped their fingers and signed themselves before going into church. With the discouragement of this practice at the Reformation, stoups were no longer required in the porch. Of the many churches that still possess stoups in their porches, two have been selected for special mention because they are of unusual interest and importance. Both churches are in Wales, Llanafan Fawr in Powys, Skenfrith in Gwent. The church at Llanafan Fawr, which is three miles south-west of Newbridge-on-Wye, was carefully restored and much reduced in size a hundred years ago. Nothing remains of the earliest building there, which probably dated back to the earliest years of the Christian church in Wales. Evidence of an early Christian connection in these parts is provided by a pillar stone of the seventh to the ninth century, which is at present lodged in the chancel. Aerial photography reveals that the present church and its very large churchyard occupy only a small part of a great circular enclosure. This enclosure and the presence on the east wall of the porch of a stone with a spiral decoration suggest the possibility of a prehistoric settlement there. Also in the east wall of this porch is a well-preserved stoup.

The other Welsh church referred to with a stoup is at Skenfrith, on the west bank of the river Monnow, about seven miles north of Monmouth; its dedication to St. Bridget, a sixth century Irish saint, suggests a much earlier church than the present one, which was built in the thirteenth century at the same time as its close neighbour, a Norman castle. This castle at Skenfrith, along with White Castle and the great keep at Grosmont, provided a stout forward defence to Monmouth in the middle ages. The south porch of this church, presided over by a stone carving of St. Bridget above the outer door, gives access to a border church of very great historical interest. Today church and castle and river combine to make this small and quite unspoiled village a place of unusual serenity and peace.

Apart from the variety of religious uses to which the porch was put there was too a multiplicity of secular practice. Parish council meetings wre held there; hence the need for considerable seating accommodation. The lord of the manor may at one time have presided but more often the presiding official was the lord's nominee, the priest. The findings of their deliberations were posted on the notice board which is still a feature of the church porch; it is pleasing to note the continuity of historical tradition here even though most of today's announcements are of rather a humdrum nature.

In those porches where there was an altar, legal contracts could be sworn, while executors of wills normally used the porch for paying out legacies to beneficiaries. The porch too was regarded as a suitable place for the payment of debts because witnesses who were essential in such transactions were easy to obtain in this most public of places. For this same reason unidentified corpses were sometimes laid out there in the expectation that someone might be able to solve the mystery; here, too, coroners held their courts. Parish stocks were often kept in the porch, when not in use and even occasionally when actually in use; examples of this practice have been cited at St. Ives and elsewhere in Cornwall. At Aberedw, up the Wye from Builth Wells in Powys, where the entrance to the church is through the north door, the benches in the porch are fourteen feet long. In this immense porch much of the legal business and trade of the parish was in former times carried on and at times of feasting and festivity village musicians used to sit on these benches and accompany the villagers on their violins as they danced under the yew trees in the churchyard just outside the porch.

In some areas the porch, in the absence of a more suitable location, had to serve as a schoolroom and also as a place where travelling pedlars in bad weather might set out their wares. Churchwardens' accounts in various parts of Norfolk bear witness to yet another use to which the church porch was sometimes put. In 1687 at Diss money was paid "to the wench Eleanor that lay in the church porch at several times." She was presumably a pauper. Elsewhere are to be found references indicating that poor people who fell on hard times and who were in consequence evicted from their cottages received temporary housing in the porch; in a Christian country the church porch was surely a suitable place of refuge in such an emergency.

Frequent examples of another use to which the church door could be put can still be seen in the presence of arrow marks in the stone work. As the men of the parish left church after morning service they sharpened their arrows and the depth of some of these grooves give a vivid reminder of this eager Sunday morning adjournment to the butts. Such reminders can still be seen in innumerable church porches. Two such church porches will here be described, one at Audlem in Cheshire, the other at Lydbury North in south Shropshire. Audlem is a small but busy town in south Cheshire, its church on a hill dominating the settlement it serves. It has a large fourteenth century porch, which was remodelled a century later. The stone seats of the original porch, which were rebuilt into the later one, possess deep grooves, where spears and swords were sharpened. Lydbury North, three miles south-east of Bishop's Castle in neighbouring Shropshire, is a quiet place today but in its long history since Offa in 792 gave the manor to the Bishop of Hereford it has known stirring times, to which the fifteenth century porch of its Norman church bears triple witness. The stone pillars on both sides of the outer doorway have deeply incised arrow grooves while the massive oak door still shows bullet holes, dating from the Civil war which passed that way in the seventeenth century. Facing the porch today is a memorial to the men of the village who lost their lives in the two world wars that have scarred the twentieth century. On both lists of dead appear the names of the Earls of Powys, whose forebears succeeded Robert Clive in the ownership of Walcot, the local mansion which was built for the hero of Plassey in the 1760s.

Seeing that the unconsecrated nave was the chief meeting place of the parish it seems highly likely that the seats in the porch fulfilled the same function that a park bench does in our society, namely that of providing a place where a man could sit and watch the passing scene, chat with his friends or just sit and stare. Some people in the past, it seems, even sat in the church porch at night, but for a special purpose, suggested by John Aubrey in the seventeenth and by Kilvert in the nineteenth century. Aubrey, who lamenting the changes brought about by the civil war in seventeenth century England and the subsequent Puritan victory wrote:—"It was a custom (i.e before the war had given the Puritans a chance to change the old order) for some people that were more curious than ordinary to sit all night in the porch of their parish church on Midsummer Eve and they should see the apparitions of those that should die in the parish that year come and knock at the door." More than two hundred years later Kilvert, the diarist of the southern Marches, noted that according to one of his parishioners at Clyro in Powys on All Hallow E'en some parishoners "used to go to the church door at midnight to hear the Saints within call over the names of those who were to die within the year."

AUDLEM

Illustrated here is the fourteenth century porch of St. James' church, Audlem in south Cheshire. On the stone bench on its east wall may be seen the deep grooves made by spears and swords. In the foreground is the stumped medieval churchyard cross on which in the eighteenth century a horizontal sundial was superimposed. On one of the buttresses on the south wall of the nave is a medieval scratch dial, which is now enclosed and thus protected from any further erosion by the elements.

CLUN

This photograph of St. George's church shows the
impressive double-storeyed porch, whose upper room
was used by the priest before coming into service as a
school. Much of the church is Norman, including the
stout tower with its pyramidal roof. Clun, with at one
end of the hilly town a Norman castle, which Pevsner
called ''a spectacular ruin'', and a Norman church on
another hill at the other end gives the impression of
having been anything but a quiet place in the Middle
Ages.

GUILSFIELD

Guilsfield, whose Welsh name is Cegidfa, was an early Christian settlement, associated with a sixth century Celtic missionary, Aelhaiarn to whom the church is dedicated. The present church, which is by no means the first to be built on that site, dates mostly from the fourteenth century and stands in a large, circular churchyard, bounded by many huge and ancient yew trees.

Shown in the illustration is the two-storeyed porch, to which was added on the west side in the eighteenth century a hearse house. The upper storey, as at Clun, was the priest's room before serving as a school room; inside the porch, which possesses a stoup, there is an immense iron-bound oak chest, hewn out of a log. It measures seven feet six inches in length and is comparable with the well-known chest in St. Beuno's church at Clynnog Fawr, in the Lleyn Peninsula.

ST. BRIDGET'S CHURCH, SKENFRITH

At Skenfrith, which is three miles south of Grosmont,
is another of the castles of the Trilateral. Nearby, also
on the banks of the Monnow, is an ancient Celtic
religious site, which was later built upon by the same
masons who erected the castle.

A striking feature of the church is the huge pyramid-
shaped tower, which can be seen on many churches
on the border between England and Wales. Such
sturdy towers offered both accommodation and
protection for parishioners when their lives were put
at risk by border raids. The Skenfrith tower has slits
which catered for the needs of doves, which provided
a supply of fresh food for those shut up down below.
In the east wall of the porch is a well-preserved stoup.

LLANBADARN FAWR

The present church, which lies about two miles north
of Llandrindod Wells in Powys, was almost entirely
rebuilt just over a hundred years ago, but it is
surrounded by a circular churchyard which proclaims
the great age of the site, to which also the tympanum
here illustrated attests. This remarkable carving over
the south door is late Norman and almost certainly
was the handiwork of the Herefordshire School of
Craftsmen, who left their glorious if irreligious marks
on Kilpeck and many other churches in the Marches.
In the south wall of this same porch is a stone,
inscribed in Latin, which probably came from the
Roman camp at Castell Collen, two miles away.

BURFORD

To the discriminating student Burford church is well-known but it is its three-tiered porch, the rich array of eighteenth century tombstones and the knowledge of a seventeenth century tragedy played out in the churchyard that particularly claim the attention of the interested layman.

On the outside of the south wall of the nave is a plaque, commemorating what took place in 1649, when a victorious Cromwell found himself faced with a local mutiny. He locked up in the church four hundred soldiers, from whose ranks he selected three for execution in the churchyard, which their fellows, one of whom carved his name on the font, watched from the church tower.

CIRENCESTER

This quite magnificent porch, which is probably the largest and finest of all church porches, was in the past frequently put to a number of secular uses.

2. THE SIGNIFICANCE OF YEW TREES

Any study that concerns itself with the significance of yew trees should start by having recourse to the prehistoric record. In the Bronze Age, for example, yew trees seem frequently to have been planted on round barrows. Yews are slow-growing trees and very long-lived so that a yew that still grows on a Bronze Age site could be a seedling from the parent tree, planted there in prehistoric times. Why yews should have been planted there still has no satisfactory explanation unless credence is given to the theory expounded by *Guy Underwood*, who in his *PATTERNS OF THE PAST* suggested that all early burial places were sited above underground springs of water and theorised that early Man marked these sites by planting yews.

Be that as it may, the yew tree played an important role in many early cultures and probably had a magic connotation. Certainly circles of yew trees were credited with possessing magic powers, though whether the power was thought to come from the trees or from their formation in a circle is impossible to know. Early man may have believed that a circle of yews gave protection and it may be that such a circle in a place of burial was believed capable of affording protection to the dead from evil spirits.

In the Britain that Augustine came to in 597 A.D. circles or semi-circles of yews would have been a familiar sight; some of these groups would have survived from the Bronze Age while others will have been in enclosures devoted to pre-Christian and therefore pagan religious rites. Four years after Augustine's mission began the Pope sent a letter to the Abbot Mellitus, who had been sent to continue Augustine's work. This letter, according to Bede, advised Christian missionaries in eastern Britain to be circumspect in their treatment of newly-converted pagans. Their temples should clearly be re-consecrated as Christian churches, whenever possible, but some pagan practices should be allowed to continue in the hope that a tolerant attitude would lead to a greater number of converts. It is quite possible that in this way yew trees may have become respectable in Christian eyes.

In addition early Christians often buried their dead in places that had previously been made sacred by prehistoric burials and in so doing would often have seen yew trees there and come to associate them with death and burial. At Guilsfield, in Powys, there is a complete circle of yew trees surrounding the church within the boundaries of a circular churchyard; there was a Christian settlement here as early as in the sixth century. Further south in Powys, at Llanfihangel-nant-Melan and at nearby Llansantffraed-in-Elvel impressive segments of circles of yews suggest at least the likelihood of there having been prehistoric burials near the present churches. Again, in an immense circular churchyard at Cwmdu, in remote country between Brecon and Abergavenny, there is a huge arc of yews.

There must be relatively few really old churchyards in the country that do not contain a yew tree. No study of yew trees could be considered complete without reference being paid to those that flourish at Painswick in Gloucestershire, where no fewer than ninety-nine carefully-tended specimens provide a fitting background to a remarkable collection of table and pedestal tombs. Yews are most

37

likely to be seen on the south side of the church, though they have been planted elsewhere in the churchyard, and anyway birds are not known to be careful only to carry seeds to consecrated ground! Although the incidence of yews is so wide-spread there is strangely enough no general agreement about why these trees should have been preferred to others. Christians as well as connecting them with death and burial may also have associated them with resurrection because of the tree's evergreen appearance. *Sir Thomas Browne*, the distinguished seventeenth century scholar and antiquary, thought about this in his *HYDRIOTAPHIA*. He wrote:— ''Whether the planting of yew in churchyards held not its original from ancient funeral rites or as an emblem of resurrection from its perpetual verdure, may admit conjecture.'' What cannot be denied is that whether medieval Christians regarded yews as emblems of death or evidence of resurrection, they thought them sufficiently important to go on planting them as new churchyards were consecrated. When Dafydd ap Gwilym, a prince of Wales and a very great poet, was buried in the fourteenth century in Strata Florida Abbey, a Cistercian house in Dyfed, mourners planted a yew tree over his grave, to which today's visitor may still bear testimony.

The association of yew trees with death does not only derive from their gloomy appearance and their frequent appearance in places of burial; the leaves, though not the berries, can be fatal to cattle. *Gilbert White* in his *ANTIQUITIES OF SELBORNE* comments thus:—''It may be proper to remind the unwary that the twigs and leaves (of the yew), though eaten in very small quantities, will kill horses and cows very quickly.'' He went on to add the strange fact that sheep and turkeys and apparently deer could crop the tree with impunity. The juice, as Shakespeare indicated, was fatal to a king, when administered by Hamlet's uncle. It may also be recalled that the witches' cauldron in Macbeth received ''slips of yew, slivered on the moon's eclipse.'' Indeed the danger that was thought to exist for cattle in the foliage of the yew may even have encouraged priests to increase the number of yew trees in their churchyards. This served to deter those farmers, who, unmindful of their obligation to keep churchyard walls and fences in a good state of repair, may have yielded to the temptation to let their cattle stray across ill-maintained boundaries in order to take advantage of lush grazing available on the south side of the church. By planting additional yews the priest was thus not only stopping cattle from grazing on consecrated ground but also ensuring that his churchyard fences would be better looked after in future.

Yew trees in churchyards, whatever their origin, from quite early Christian times, have been made to serve a useful purpose; according to the Book of Llandaff the right of sanctuary in Wales was granted to those who sought refuge ''between the yew tree and the church door.'' From early Saxon times in England clusters of yews were used as stockades within which frightened villagers in times of danger could store their wordly goods and find sanctuary. The blessings that the yew in this protecting role conferred upon the harassed and the tormented were commemorated by Walter de la Mare in these verses:—

Of all the trees in England
Oak, Elder, Elm and Thorn,
The Yew alone burns lamps of peace
For them that lie forlorn.''

Sometimes yew trees were planted in churchyards in order to provide a ready-to-hand supply of raw material for the making of bows; it is indeed true that many early churches were of necessity sturdily built and occupied key defensive positions, which sometimes had to withstand sudden attack so that many a bow would probably have been made in a hurry from a yew tree conveniently close at hand. English bowmen in their heyday in the middle ages, however, tended to import yew from abroad, especially from Spain, preferring it to the home-grown wood, while the bowmen of south-east Wales, who were regarded as the best in the Principality, made their bows from elm. Nevertheless as late as in the sixteenth century in some areas yew trees still formed a part of the parson's freehold, in consequence of which the local militia was often supplied. This source of revenue was soon to dry up, for in 1595 the Privy Council decreed that bows should never again be issued as weapons of war, although there seems to have been some delay in banning the use of the bow in sport. (*Trevelyan* in his *ENGLISH SOCIAL HISTORY* mentioned the unhappy fate that befell a game-keeper in 1621, when he was shot by mistake when the Archbishop of Canterbury was aiming at a buck!)

In 1307 Edward I decreed that clumps of yews should be planted in churchyards near church doors in order to protect the buildings from high winds and storms, a course of action much commended in the eighteenth century by Gilbert White. Yew trees in the middle ages came to play an important part also in the preparation for Easter; on Ash Wednesday in parts of Cheshire and elsewhere in the Marches the foreheads of the faithful were smeared with the ashes of yew. Its greater importance however was seen on Palm Sunday, on which day in every church a procession went round the churchyard. In the absence of palm leaves a substitute had to be found; normally hazel catkins were called into use but the climate was as eccentric as the date of Easter with the result that in some years on Palm Sunday the hazel catkins were not properly out and in other years they were already past their best. Hence quite frequently sprigs of yew had pride of place in the Palm Sunday processions.

Away from the world of the church and churchyard, those who dabbled in magic in the middle ages preferred to make their wands of yew and from quite early historic times in Ireland the yew was found to make the most sensitive divining rods. Centuries ago in the north of England, when something precious was lost, the loser was thought to have the best chance of recovering the lost treasure if he cut down a branch of yew and carried it in front of him while he searched.

Two hundred years ago in the Marches the vicar of Beguildy, in the eastern part of Powys, just west of Offa's Dyke, was credited with availing himself of the powers of magic. The occasion was a fight between the unbeaten champion of those parts, who hailed from Newtown, and the challenger from Llanbadarn Fynydd, a village not far from Beguildy. The Newtown man was thoroughly beaten, to the astonishment of all the bystanders until, according to an alleged eye-witness, the explanation became apparent. The vicar was discovered nearby "sitting in a yew tree, with a huge book opened in front of him, directing the evil spirits to assist the Llanbadarn man."

It still appears even in the twentieth century that a little of the old magic stays with the tree. For in some parts it is still thought unlucky to cut down a yew tree in a churchyard, while in outlying hamlets in Brittany the old belief lingers on that the churchyard yew sends down a root into the mouth of every corpse. Even as recently as twenty years ago in the Forest of Dean in Gloucestershire children were warned not to speak when they walked under a certain yew in the churchyard through fear of something terrible happening to them—evidence of residual magic even in the nuclear age!

At Chorlton-on-Otmoor in Oxforshire a cross of yew stands above the rood screen in the church and on May Day it is decorated with flowers, a splendid instance of the fusion of pagan and Christian practices, which might have appealed to that Pope who had counselled his early missionaries in these islands to compromise, where no vital principles were involved.

While it is invidious to particularise, it can be said without fear of contradiction that in the following thirty churchyards in the Midlands, West and North-West, and in Wales there are immensely old yew trees:—

Aberedw, Acton Scott, Alderley, Astbury, Baschurch, Bawdry, Bredwardine, Bucknell, Cascob, Church Preen, Claverley, Disserth, Glascwm, Guilsfield, Hope Bagot, Kilpeck, Llanbadarn Garreg, Llanbister, Llanelltud, Llanfihangel-ar-arth, Maentwrog, Meidrim, Moccas, Montgomery, Nevern, Old Radnor, Partrishow, Pennant Melangell, Rhulen and Skenfrith.

LLANFIHANGEL-NANT-MELAN

A number of churches dedicated to St. Michael are to
be found in the district around the Radnor Forest,
because in early times a dragon was thought to inhabit
these wild hills. St. Michael, with his record of having
driven Lucifer out of Heaven, had acquired a
reputation for dealing successfully with the likes of
dragons! (It is interesting to note that there are three
times as many churches dedicated to St. Michael in
Wales, a predominantly hilly country, as there are in
England)
The church, which, like the village itself, was the
concern of St. Michael, was built on a mound within a
ring of yews, of which eight still stand. Early
Christians probably chose to settle in this place
because it had already been made sacred by their
predecessors in the Bronze Age, who buried their dead
in a round barrow, which they protected by a circle of
yews.

STRATA FLORIDA

This splendid and flourishing yew tree stands in the very middle of the grave of Dafydd ap Gwilym; today his grave is surrounded by the graves of those buried in after years in the churchyard of the local church. When the poet died, however, in the fourteenth century, this area was in the grounds of the abbey, whose well-tended ruins are now separated from it by a stout wall.

CWMDU

St. Michael's church, Cwmdu lies between the Brecon Beacons and the Black Mountains to the north-west of Abergavenny. In the foreground of the illustration are the remains of a medieval churchyard cross and behind it are two of the twenty-four yew trees, which are dotted around the periphery of an exceptionally large church-yard.

On one of the south buttresses of the church is a pillar stone, commemorating in Latin a Christian burial of the late sixth or early seventh century, while, propped up in the porch of the priest's door, is another early memorial stone, bearing a ringed cross.

PAINSWICK

This large and beautiful churchyard at Painswick in
the southern Cotswolds is outstanding for its
tombstones of a rare richness and for its many clipped
yews, most of which were planted when the tombs
were erected in the eighteenth century.

3. SANCTUARY IN CHURCH AND CHURCHYARD

What today is often referred to as the conflict between church and state is in essence a realisation that material and non-material interests may pull in opposite directions. Quite early on in historical times there seems to have developed a general awareness that there was no real community of interest between the material and the spiritual. The former tolerated the latter as long as it made no attempt to steal its thunder, while the spiritual tended to put up with the material provided that there was no gross infringement of what it regarded as being basically right. When, however, there was a clash of interests the odds greatly favoured the secular power, which had the means of enforcing its decisions. Nevertheless the rulers for a variety of reasons generally kept their hands off the actual shrines where religious power seemed to be concentrated. In Greek literature Aeschylus made Orestes immune from arrest, once he had found sanctuary in the temple of Pallas Athene in Athens. The idea gradually found acceptance in the pre-Christian world that fugitives from justice could escape arrest as long as they stayed in holy precincts.

With the coming of Christianity the problem came to a head, especially when those enjoying political power themselves became Christians. Such rulers had to recognise that the altar in a Christian church was a holy place and that the priest who served his religion there was a holy man. From the acceptance of that position it was no great step to agree that any man who came within the ambience of that altar was thought, as long as he remained there, to have acquired something of the sacredness of that place. In consequence it would be regarded as an act of sacrilege for anyone, however powerful, to break into a Christian church and forcibly to remove that man, even though there was very good reason to believe that he had broken the law of that land.

The Christian church officially recognised the right of sanctuary in 399 A.D. and twenty years later extended the privilege to a distance of fifty paces from the door of the church. In 431 the area was more closely defined to contain all the land surrounding the church, in other words the churchyard. This extension was decided on to save the possible defilement of the church, which was thought likely to take place if fugitives were allowed to eat and sleep in the actual building. Thus the churchyard joined the church in providing a refuge. The first known reference to sanctuary in these islands came in about 600, when Ethelbert, King of Kent, whose Christian wife had converted him and made him receptive to Augustine's mission, in a general statement of existing religious practices in the Christian church clearly confirmed the right of sanctuary. At first sanctuary was permissible for a limited time only, to enable the authorities an opportunity to bring about some settlement or in some cases possibly to prevent any personal vengeance from being taken.

From very early times then the church and the churchyard were regarded as places of temporary refuge, but not only for those who were fleeing the law but also for those who were the victims of brigandage or raids from rapacious neighbours. In those troubled, unsettled days sanctuary was probably far more important to society as a means of affording protection to the helpless and innocent than as a temporary buffer between the felon and the law. It was no uncommon occurrence for a churchyard to provide virtual storage facilities for household goods and even cattle as well as sanctuary for their owners. At this time plain crosses were sometimes put up at crossroads in parts of Saxon England on which the one word Sanctuarium was inscribed, to serve as a signpost to guide a fugitive to the nearest place of refuge. In later Saxon days, as government became more centralised and law and order better organised, this sanctuary in church and churchyard became less a place of refuge for victims of local raids and more the temporary resort of those who had fallen foul of those in authority. In general before the Norman conquest the immunity given by the church lasted up to nine days, that period of time being thought sufficient for both parties to cool down and come to a sensible arrangement.

With the Normans on the throne there were more detailed rules and regulations for sanctuary. In 1070 William made it clear that sanctuary, though only temporary, could be extended to forty days; during that period the refugee was free to make a private arrangement with his persecutor. If however he failed to satisfy him, when the forty days expired, he had to appear before the coroner and, what is more, he had to appear in sackcloth. This court would usually have taken place in the porch of the church. There he was expected to confess his crimes and "abjure the realm," that is, swear on oath to leave the country. The refugee was then guaranteed a safe passage out of the country, provided that he wore a white robe to distinguish him, that he carried a wooden cross, that he kept to the main roads and that he spent not more than two nights in any one place. The time allowance was far from generous; for instance in the reign of Edward III the walk from Yorkshire to Dover had to be accomplished in nine days.

Not all the felons in sanctuary took advantage of these terms with the result that a century later by the Assize of Northampton in 1170 those who outstayed the legal limit of forty days were to be forced "to abjure the realm." There seems to have been some fear that as the forty days were drawing to a close the fugitive might try to escape from sanctuary to avoid having to go abroad. In some cases church and churchyard were guarded day and night and there is even a case on record of trenches being dug outside a churchyard wall to keep a fugitive in sanctuary!

Although the need for sanctuary seems to have been a real and growing one in the early middle ages, written records of it are few and far between because by the time that there were churchwardens' accounts the need for sanctuary had largely passed. Visual reminders of sanctuary may still occasionally be seen in country churches here and there. There is a well-worn sanctuary ring on the south door of the little white church of Rhulen, in a remote corner of Powys, and a sanctuary knocker on the south door of the church at Cound, in Shropshire, while further south in the same county the earliest reference to there being a parish church at all at Woolstaston near Craven Arms is contained in a tantalisingly brief note that the church there in 1272 was used as a sanctuary by felons. At Greystoke in Cumbria a hundred yards outside the church gates is a medieval sanctuary stone, now built into the outside wall of a swimming bath; this stone originally marked the boundary beyond which fugitives could claim sanctuary. However the enquirer is on firmer ground where the written record is concerned when consideration is given to churchyards being specially consecrated in order to provide sanctuary for a district. In Herefordshire the monks of the great minster at Leominster had a very large area under their jurisdiction; in the course of time they agreed to a church being built at Hampton, a settlement some three miles to the south of the town. Here, as so often happened when permission to build a church was given in this manner, no arrangement was made for a churchyard to be marked out around the church. Many years later, in the twelfth century, the Bishop of Hereford, with the agreement of the monks of Leominster, consecrated a churchyard around the church at Hampton, which was to be available "as a place of refuge", in return for which thereafter an annual payment was made to the monks of Leominster.

Further west in Wales, although there were proper and regionally different arrangements for sanctuary (i.e. "between the yew tree and the church door," according to the Book of Llandaff), the times appear to have been less troubled. Giraldus Cambrensis, writing in about 1200, reported:—"The churches in Wales are more quiet and tranquil than those elsewhere. Around them the cattle graze peacefully not only in the churchyards

but outside too within the fences and ditches marked out and set by bishops to fix the sanctuary limits." The Archdeacon went on to say that the more important churches offered more sanctuary still, for as far as "the cattle go to feed in the morning and return in the evening," a privilege which apparently was sometimes grossly abused.

It would be as well here to make some mention of another type of sanctuary that had come into existence in Norman times. When in 1070 William confirmed the general right of sanctuary which belonged to every parish church, he also decreed that there should be a special sanctuary available in certain places, which would require a royal charter. In general these special places were abbeys and cathedrals, of which there were twenty-two named, where sanctuary could be—and indeed often was—for life. In the centuries that followed some of these life-refugees became the bane of their unwilling hosts, who were forced to maintain them. Many bitter complaints, most of them probably quite justified, were made from time to time about the alleged rogues who used "ecclesiastical precincts as bases for systematic robbery." Westminster Abbey seems to have been particularly unfortunate in this respect, so much so that the phrase "taking Westminster" came to have a very special meaning.

After the end of the middle ages little attention was paid to sanctuary, the rules governing it being considerably tightened up thereafter. Henry VIII in 1529 made life more unpleasant for those abjuring the realm by ordering coroners to brand all those in sanctuary with the letter A on the back of the thumb on their right hands before letting them set out for the coast. In 1540 the privilege of sanctuary was abolished for those believed guilty of murder, rape, burglary, highway robbery or arson, while in 1623 James I virtually abolished the right of sanctuary altogether, though in fact in a few places sanctuary for debt was allowed until well into the nineteenth century.

An interesting attempt to revive the right of sanctuary was reported in the summer of 1985. A Greek Cypriot couple who escaped from Cyprus when their part of the island was occupied by Turkish troops, had settled in London but without the necessary papers. When this omission was discovered, the couple fled to a London church where they successfully claimed sanctuary for a short while until their luck ran out and a reluctant Home Secretary forced them to return to Cyprus.

ST. DAVID'S CHURCH, RHULEN

To the privileged few who manage to reach the little
white church up a long and narrow lane under the
rounded hills of Radnorshire, the reward will be great.
Here man and nature have combined to produce
something rather special. Today's church, dating from
the early Middle Ages, stands on a hill, its rounded
and very large churchyard sprinkled with massive
yews; the first foundation here was probably no more
than a flimsy hut of wattle and daub, where a few
hardy Celtic monks lived and prayed and carried out
the instructions of the clas at Glascwm. On the south
door is a well-worn sanctuary ring; outside in the
Spring the churchyard is alight with daffodils.

49

4.   CHURCHYARD CROSSES

Of all the links with the past still to be seen in old churchyards none is worth greater study than the crosses; although today's survivals rarely go back beyond the fourteenth century, even these crosses represent a tradition that dates from the very first Christian settlements on sanctified ground. For in very early times, that is in the sixth and seventh centuries, Christian missionaries, having selected a suitable site for worship, erected a wooden cross; if the mission proved successful and a local connection was made, Christian burials would in the fulness of time have been grouped around this cross. When later still a church was built, it would normally have been so sited that its shadow would not have fallen upon the cross. This is one reason why so many medieval churches stand nearer the north than the southern wall of the churchyard. The first crosses then had been set up originally to mark early Christian sites well before any building was planned. Such crosses acted as Christian markers around which Christian burials would later have taken place. The heads of these crosses are likely to have been simply cruciform unless they were in Northumbria, where the wheelhead predominated or in Wales, where the thirteen foot high cross in the south side of the churchyard at Nevern in Dyfed furnishes an outstanding example of a Celtic Cross.

Whether these crosses were quite separate and different from preaching crosses is far from clear; certainly early missionaries caused preaching crosses to be set up, as happened in Wales in very early times indeed. One of the earliest and certainly one of the most striking crosses dating from the ninth century still survives in the churchyard at St. Canna's Church at Llangan in Glamorgan. Preaching crosses, later of stone, continued to be erected in churchyards well into the Middle Ages, some of them coming to be associated with the Crusades. Many a cross had a small niche in the shaft to hold the pyx, inside which was the host; an excellent example of this is to be seen in the churchyard at Weobley, a black and white market town in north Herefordshire.

Yet another type of cross was erected in medieval churchyards and that was a market cross. It has to be remembered that although the south side of the churchyard was consecrated ground, for many centuries most of it was not required for burials. Furthermore, to medieval man there was nothing improper about the idea of conducting business on consecrated ground. Such a location on the contrary was thought to provide a safe guarantee of fair trading and honest undertakings.

No matter what the origin of the churchyard cross, whether it had been erected to mark a holy site, a missionary enterprise or a trading point, existing crosses in the Middle Ages were used for a variety of purposes, religious and secular. Certainly on special occasions in the church calendar, such as Saints' Days, the crosses occupied key positions on processional routes, while on Palm Sunday, when the greatest of church processions took place, the Gospel was read from its steps. Sometimes, too, sermons were preached there. In addition, of course, so long as the law of the land allowed, buying and selling went on around the market cross, from whose steps also on special occasions public proclamations were made. The significance of some of these proclamations seems to have lessened considerably in later years; evidence exists of Sunday morning announcements after service being made there by churchwardens, in the eighteenth century and later, on such trivial matters as the current reward being offered for the destruction of foxes and hedgehogs.

Came the Reformation in the sixteenth century and with it the widespread mutilation of churchyard crosses, which were thought by religious reformers to be too closely associated with old ways of thinking to be allowed to survive into the brave new world of Protestant zealots. The Tudors dealt savagely with these crosses; those which escaped destruction in this way were truncated in the following century by an act of Parliament which limited the height of a shaft to four feet six inches. However by a happy coincidence at about this time the ancient method of marking the time by a vertical sun-dial scratched on the south wall of the church was succeeded by a better type of sun-dial which was horizontal. It is not therefore surprising that a great many of these truncated shafts were given a new lease of life by having horizontal marker plates built into their tops, at the very convenient height of four feet and six inches above the ground! To this day numerous seventeenth and eighteenth century sun-dials will be seen to be supported by the truncated shafts of medieval crosses.

In the Midlands and in the Marches, there are traces in many church-yards of medieval crosses, though in some places the evidence is vestigial, amounting to little more than the steps and the base from which in post-Reformation times the shafts were unceremoniously wrenched away. In northern parts of the area, more particularly in Cheshire, will still be found many truncated shafts, which were subsequently capped with horizontal sun-dials in the seventeenth or early eighteenth centuries; good examples in the county may be seen at Alderley, Bosley, Lower Peover, Prestbury and Tilston. Sun-dials, mounted on old crosses, may also be seen further south, especially in Shropshire and Herefordshire, but further south these conversions become rarer. In England and Wales as a whole, despite sixteenth century bigotry and seventeenth century legislation, some medieval crosses have survived more or less intact, though the best remaining examples tend to be found in the areas farthest removed from the seat of Government in London.

On both sides of the border, however, both north and south there are plenty of ruined medieval crosses still to be seen in the sorry state in which their mutilators left them. In saying that there are certainly fifty of them there, the author is aware of having left many churchyards unvisited and therefore the possibility must exist of there being even more, with some well-preserved specimens going unrecorded. A few outstanding examples will have to speak for all. Those chosen are at Astbury in Cheshire, at Alberbury in Shropshire, at Garway and Welsh Newton in Herefordshire, at Grosmont in Gwent and, keeping the best to last, at Partrishow in Powys.

Astbury, in east Cheshire, a short distance south of Congleton, has had a church since the seventh century, although the present one was built in the thirteenth and enlarged in the fifteenth century. The churchyard cross is—unusually—on the north side of the churchyard, prompting the thought that it was originally erected as a preaching cross. After the statutory truncation of the shaft took place in the seventeenth century, a horizontal sun-dial was placed on top of it, bearing the inscription Tempus fugit, James Green fecit; the three original steps, which are said by some to symbolise faith, hope and charity, have been worn down by the tread of ages. This particular sun-dial will have been of very limited value as a time-keeper as for a portion of every day the church will have stood between it and the rays of the sun.

Alberbury in Shropshire is very near the boundary with Powys; at the beginning of the nineteenth century George IV, when Prince of Wales is said, when staying at the great house in Loton Park in the village, to have walked the mile into Wales, bringing back with him a sprig of oak picked from the first tree he passed over the border. This tree still bears a plaque, proclaiming it to be The Prince's Oak. On the south side of Alberbury's very large fortress church, with its saddleback thirteenth century tower, is a medieval cross, which has now been given a modern shaft, surmounted by three sun-dials. The church, which has seen more alteration than most in its long history, once possessed a porch, in which Old Parr, as has already been told, once did penance, when a hundred years old.

The inclusion of Garway on this list is prompted by the desire to lure visitors to this remote but remarkable church in south-west Herefordshire, not far from the river Monnow, which at this point marks the boundary between England and Wales. South of the church stands a sun-dial, itself built into an old quern which is supported by the shaft of a medieval cross. St. Michael's church is a strong border church with an immense and once separate tower to act as fortress; in addition it contains a chapel which belonged to the Knights Templar, which in later days passed into the hands of the Knights of St. John of Jerusalem. The outside wall of this chapel reveals a number of well-preserved incised crosses of various patterns all associated with medieval orders of military knights. All this and much more is there to be wondered at in this hidden corner of Archenfield, formerly a Celtic island in a Mercian sea.

A few miles south-east of Garway, and still in the magic land of Archenfield, is Welsh Newton; the church, which lies up a secluded green lane off the main road, acted as a chapel of ease to Garway and thus had associations with the Knights Templar. A medieval cross once dominated the south side of the churchyard; today the ancient steps remain but the shaft and head are modern. Beneath the cross are two graves, one of a medieval knight, the other of the luckless John Kemble, who in 1679 paid with his life for holding mass in a private house.

Partrishow church—there is no village—is perched on a hillside four and a half miles north-east of Crickhowell. So very remote is this church that twice in its long history authority has failed to have its way. Three altars, bearing consecration crosses, still survive despite the prohibition of Edward VI, which Elizabeth repeated, and in the churchyard, just south-east of the porch stands a medieval cross with its shaft still miraculously complete, thanks to the inability of the parliamentary commissioners in the seventeenth century to penetrate these hills. The lantern above the shaft, though quite modern, seems appropriate.

NEVERN

St. Brynach's church in Nevern occupies a sixth century site and is particularly famous for its sixth century Christian memorial stones, both inside the church and in the churchyard. In the present context however attention is drawn to a tall stone, erected several centuries later; this carved cross, which, unlike the two other well-known Celtic crosses in Wales, stands in a churchyard. The circumstances of its erection are unknown but experts place it in the tenth century. Its purpose too is not entirely clear, though it may well have been set up to commemorate a holy place, associated with the founder of the first church on the site, St. Brynach, the sixth century friend of St. David himself. The great avenue of ancient yew trees in the churchyard should also be noted.

GARWAY

PARTRISHOW

The church (there is no village) is situated up a steep and very narrow lane, west of the Grwyne Fawr in Powys, in the south-west corner of the Black Mountains. It does not easily yield up its treasures but to those who persevere there comes a real reward. Its very isolation protects it still, as it did in the past, when parliamentary commissioners were unable to find their way and were thus prevented from carrying out the orders of their masters in London. Hence Partrishow still has altars with consecration crosses and still has in its churchyard a medieval preaching cross with its shaft rising to its original height. To this cross came Archbishop Baldwin, accompanied by his chaplain and chronicler, Giraldus Cambrensis and here he proclaimed the Third Crusade in 1188, his audience assembled on the stone seat that runs along the outside of the church.

St. Michael's church at Garway in south-west Herefordshire was designed as a fortress with a solid tower built separately, occupying its main line of defence. In the seventeenth century a short stone passage joined the tower to the rest of the church; this is still referred to locally at "The Prison", suggesting its probable use.

In the neighbouring farmyard is an early fourteenth century dove-cot, which provided house-room for six hundred and sixty-six birds; it bears an inscription that indicates that it was the work of the Knights Templars, whose original round church at Garway was later built over by the Knights Hospitallers. The shaft of the medieval cross, shown in the photograph, was truncated by Act of Parliament in the seventeenth century and now supports a sun-dial, which was superimposed in the eighteenth century. At its base is an old quern.

ST. NICHOLAS' CHURCH, GROSMONT

After the Conquest the victorious William embarked upon an ambitious programme of trying to impose his will upon Wales. His representative in Hereford, having chosen Monmouth as a suitable site for a castle, completed its outer defences by building three more fortifications which became known as the Trilateral. The most northerly of these was at Grosmont, whose geographical setting is implicit in its Norman-French name. Here a castle was built on the hill that overlooks the Monnow, a garrison established to man it and at the bottom of the hill a church to cater for the spiritual needs of the garrison. The north side of the churchyard at Grosmont, contrary to normal practice, was consecrated, where may still be seen the octagonal base and the shaft of an early medieval cross, stumped to the regulation height of four feet six inches and surmounted by a carved capstone, which, though undoubtedly medieval in character, must have been placed there at a much later date.

Parishioners at Grosmont today worship in the chancel, as the huge nave, which is no longer required to serve a much-contracted community, has been deconsecrated and turned into a fascinating store-house of local history.

WELSH NEWTON

CHURCHYARD CROSS, WEOBLEY

In an area, rich in preaching crosses, none is better preserved than this one in Weobley, a delightful small black and white town in north Herefordshire, which through the centuries had a castle at one end of the town (its ruins barely visible) and at the other a church with a very tall spire, set in a very large churchyard. At the base of the cross are four niches, one of which will have held the pyx that contained the Host. Especially in the Palm Sunday procession the cross played a central part; it frequently had secular significance too as traditionally important public proclamations were made from this vantage point.

Welsh Newtown is situated in that part of southern Herefordshire known as Archenfield, whose Welsh inhabitants in the early Middle Ages successfully resisted the cultural invasion of Mercian settlement. The church, in a two-acre churchyard, in which the cross illustrated stands, was built in the thirteenth century, to pass first into the care of the Knights Templars and later into that of their successors, the Knights Hospitallers.

Still to be seen on the north side of the chancel is a stone seat, specially erected as the place of authority for the representatives of the Knights Templars in Garway on their periodical visitations. In the later years of the Middle Ages this same seat acted as sanctuary for those in flight from their enemies.

In the far corner of the churchyard, this cross stands high above a jungle of weeds, that in summer obliterates the graves at its base, of a medieval knight and of John Kemble, who in 1679 was executed for saying mass in the nearby Pembridge Castle, then as now, a private house. Today this former preaching cross, which would once have played an important part in many a churchyard procession of witness, once again seems all of a piece, obscuring the fact that, while the steps and the base belong to the Middle Ages, the shaft and the cross on top of it are modern.

5. PATRONAL FEASTS, PLAYS, MARKETS AND FAIRS

At one time every church had a patronal day, a day of special rejoicing, commemorating either the dedication of the church or the birthday of the saint in whose name the church was dedicated. The inspiration for this celebration seems to have been the oft-quoted letter, which the missionary Mellitus received from Pope Gregory, when the eastern part of Britain at the beginning of the seventh century was in the early throes of being won back to Christianity. The missionary was advised not to do away with the feasting habits of the so-called pagans but rather to use them for the good of the Christian cause. Hence in place of gluttony there was to be moderate eating and drinking to the glory of God, such festivities to be closely linked with the dedication of the church or with the birthday of its chosen saint. The converted pagans were encouraged to make merry; they could erect their booths in the churchyard and make their tents there with boughs of trees and then come into the church to give thanks to God. The habit grew and became custom; on the eve of a patronal day there were candle-lit processions to the church in honour of the saint in whose name the church was dedicated. This simple religious celebration preceded a public holiday on the morrow, when the north side of the church yard, which was generally unconsecrated, became the setting for various secular diversions such as games and jousting, plays and dancing. Such a holiday offered infinite possibilities to ordinary people, whose harsh existence came to depend upon such occasions for relaxation and enjoyment, with the inevitable consequence that the religious purpose of the celebrations became swallowed up in the secular pleasures that accompanied them. Patronal feast-days seem to have led directly to parish wakes, which have sometimes been confused with church ales. *Joseph Strutt*, writing in his *SPORTS AND PASTIMES OF THE PEOPLE OF ENGLAND* in 1800 quoted a tenth century authority which revealed that abuses had already crept in. The account said:—''The people fell to lechery, and songs and dances, with harping and piping and also to gluttony and sin, and so turned the holiness to cursedness; wherefore holy fathers ordered the people to leave that waking and to fast the evening.''

The decline in religious emphasis was noted as early as in the twelfth century by Giraldus Cambrensis, who described how a priest's effort to keep the vigil of a saint's day by religious observance was quickly followed by boisterous merry making. Leaving the church to the priest to continue with his prayers the young men and women of the parish went into the churchyard, most fittingly by the north door, and spent the entire night dancing the carole, a ring dance that enjoyed great popularity in the middle ages. This very vigorous, whirling dance, which was accompanied by the excited singing of innumerable choruses, would grow to a tremendous crescendo. At dawn the weary dancers, Giraldus reported, would troop back into the church to find the devout priest still chanting his Latin office. A few years later the Bishop of Worcester repeated a diocesan ban on singing and dancing on these occasions. ''Let none come'' he ordered in 1240 ''to such vigils save for reasons of devotion and willingness to abstain from such practices.''

With patronal feasts taking place at different times, enabling people in one parish to participate in the revels of the next, Convocation in 1536, in an attempt to deal with a deteriorating situation, tried to improve things by ordering all festivities to take place everywhere on the same day, which was to be the first Sunday in October. This instruction seems to have been widely disobeyed. In the churchwardens' accounts at Lower Peover in Cheshire, more than a hundred and fifty years later, in 1698, reference is made to the ''Feast of Dedication, commonly called the Wakes'', taking place on the 5th of August, while in the Powys village of Disserth the celebration of the patronal festival was held on the first Sunday in July until the calendar was reformed in 1752, when it was put back to the second Sunday in the month. The full-blooded celebrations at Disserth, complete with games and dancing along with much eating and drinking was organised from the church porch; a visitor to the parish in 1744 was so impressed by what he saw that he wrote a report of it, which happily survives. This anonymous Shropshire lawyer had this to say about the Disserth wake. ''At the end of the mead by the river side were a company dancing in a barn . . . they were about nine couple, genteely dressed and all people of fortune and fashion . . . the best and most active country dances I ever saw . . . the men were gay and genteel, handsome and well-shaped; the women were genteel without pride, modest without affectation, beautiful without art and free without fondness. The generous hand of nature appeared in every face, unspoiled with the artful follies of this degenerate age. The churchyard, though large, was filled with people of almost all ages and qualities. On one side of the church were six couples dancing to one violin, and just below three or four couples to three violins, whose seat was on a tombstone. In short the whole was whimsically odd. We here saw common games played against the sacred pile and there also music playing over the bones of the deceased. We were in the middle of a merry, noisy throng.''

The church at Llanbister, which like Disserth is in Powys, is dedicated to a sixth century missionary, Cynllo, whose patronal day was July 17th. The celebrations, which were held on the first Sunday after that date, began with a special service in the church, which was followed by eating, drinking and dancing in the huge and hilly churchyard there. A traditional dish associated with the Llanbister wake was a rice pudding, stuffed with so many raisins that it resembled cake. Every year certain houses were nominated for the responsibility of cooking the rice puddings. On the patronal day the great pans, called steins, which held the delicacy, were carried to the churchyard, where they were placed on the wall before being cut into slices for all and sundry to help themselves, free of charge. Ale and cider were the accompanying drinks.

On the other side of Offa's Dyke, in Shropshire it was apparently the custom on the patronal day for sons and daughters who were in service to be allowed home for family reunion, thus reinforcing the custom of Mothering Sunday. At Cardington in the same county there was a half-holiday in the school and a gingerbread stall from the neighbouring village of Rushbury was set up outside St. James' church. At several places in the county a common diversion was a competition to find out which man could pull the ugliest face. A horse's collar was mounted on a pole and the contestants had to place their heads through it and grin. A popular prize was tobacco. Most patronal feasts in the county were accompanied by the sale of nuts, sweets and gingerbread on the north side of the churchyard. An advertisement in a local paper in 1777 showed that at Shawbury, a large and prosperous village, north of Shrewsbury, the festival, which took place in the middle of August, the church being dedicated to the Virgin Mary, whose day was August 15th, began with a service in the church on Sunday, followed by a play on Monday and horse races on Tuesday and Wednesday. Particular delicacies came to be associated with certain wakes; fig cakes, mintcakes and wheatcakes all had their devotees. In some villages, where the saints' days fell conveniently, there were cherry wakes, with the ripe fruit displayed for sale on the gravestones. At several places both in Shropshire and in Herefordshire, where the feasts were celebrated at the end of September, there were crab wakes. The ripe crab apples were not used, as might be expected, to make jelly but rather to provide ammunition where-with to pelt passers-by.

By the end of the eighteenth century licence generally seems to have taken over the various celebrations, so that drunkenness, bawdiness and indeed open fighting had become so common that the days of the feasts were clearly numbered.

Finally in 1837 Parliament forbade the announcement of parish wakes from the pulpit, while in 1840 the Society for the Suppression of Sunday Wakes was formed. By the end of the nineteenth century the jollifications had come to an end and the strains of music had died away from the churchyard. Despite the spread of drunken debauches in the churchyard at certain times of the years, it would be wrong to assume that all activities in the churchyard should merit similar criticism. It has to be remembered that in many villages this north side of the churchyard constituted the only meeting place and indeed many other secular activities that went on there were wholly admirable.

It should perhaps be said here that, whereas in the Middle Ages the naves of churches, which were unconsecrated, were frequently used for non-religious purposes such as church ales and parish festivities, after the Reformation attempts were sometimes made to bring back the past. Shropshire provides one such illustration. In 1637 the men of the parish of Clungunford thought themselves so badly treated by a new vicar who would not lay on a meal for them in church on Easter Day that they sent a petition to Archbishop Laud himself for the restoration of their former privilege. In their petition the parishioners drew the attention of the Archbishop to the additional fact that the congregation, many of whom lived a long way off, had spent the entire day in church. Laud reacted diplomatically; he allowed their petition, agreeing that their privilege should be restored but laid it down firmly that in future they would be allowed to enjoy their bread and cheese and beer again but only in the parsonage house, not in the church.

To return to the Middle Ages, in one sense the church at that time was a theatrical stage; the recurring drama of the mass was enacted there and the vividly-painted Biblical scenes on the walls of the nave will have acted as scenery. Against this background what are called Mystery plays slowly and separately developed until dramatic performances enshrining the stories of the Bible and more particularly the birth, life, passion and death of Christ were acted in medieval churches by the priests, who were sometimes aided and abetted in the minor roles by selected parishioners if they were deemed suitable for the responsibility. Temporary scaffolding was built in the church for these performances, which normally took place at the appropriate festivals in the church calendar, such as at Christmas and Easter. At Chester the local mystery plays in which scenes and actions from the Bible were embellished, were produced in the nave of St. Peter's church, with laymen, probably from the guilds, dressed up to represent biblical characters. It appears that in the course of time these plays became so popular that a bigger stage was required and perhaps a more sophisticated approach; in addition the attitude of the church authorities in some parts seems to have hardened against plays and players. It is known, for instance, that the Bishop of Hereford in the middle of the fourteenth century forbade the performance of any play in any church in his diocese, commenting that by these plays "the hearts of the faithful are drawn aside to vanities." At any rate these religious dramas sometime in the thirteenth century moved out of the church to be performed in the north side of the churchyard. There gradually the trade guilds made themselves responsible for the productions, taking over the acting parts previously taken by the priests. Later on these plays moved on again, when the guilds took them on movable stages into the towns and villages. Even then for some years the churchyard would sometimes have been the venue; for instance it is known that strolling players in Shropshire frequently visited Shrewsbury, where they normally put on their plays on Sundays after the hours of church service. There is a contemporary record in the sixteenth century of their movable state being erected in the churchyard of St. Chad's there.

This native liturgical drama, based on scriptural events and developed by the priests as vivid illustrations of their teaching and preaching, was greatly strengthened in the early fourteenth century, when the new festival of Corpus Christi was ordained by Rome. On the Thursday after Trinity Sunday processions were to take place throughout Christendom. The pageants that grew up on Corpus Christi Day were to give a real fillip to the development of drama here, though from such fragmentary evidence that survives it would appear that the emphasis in many places was more on gaudy pageantry than on serious drama.

That some plays continued to be acted in churches and churchyards seems certain from references to attempts made by the authorities to stop them, especially in the sixteenth century, when, for instance, Bonner, the Bishop of London, in 1542, two hundred years after the Bishop of Hereford had similarly acted, issued a proclamation to the clergy of the diocese, forbidding the performance of any play or interlude in any church under his jurisdiction.

Some of the stumped crosses, already referred to as surviving in churchyards from the middle ages, were originally market crosses around the steps of which much buying and selling took place, even in the consecrated south side of the churchyard. At one time it appears that markets tended to be part of the celebration of the patronal feasts; they were therefore not surprisingly often held on a Sunday. As the markets became more popular the powers-that-be tried to clamp down on them; for instance, in Shropshire Henry III in 1224 ordered Wenlock market to be moved from Sunday to Monday, in a move to try to loosen its ties with the church. The use of the churchyard both on the north and the south sides for markets was officially brought to an end by Edward I towards the end of the thirteenth century, when he forbade not only markets in churchyards but also the much more widely held fairs, which flourished on festive occasions on the north side. The prohibition does not however appear to have been too rigorously applied because fairs continued to be held in many places, but especially in the Welsh part of the Marches, where the churchyards rang to their noise until nearly the end of the sixteenth century.

A fair today has a changed connotation; swings and roundabouts, bright lights, noise and mechanical amusements sum up what is now meant by "all the fun of the fair." This change has taken place within the last two hundred years. In the Middle Ages amusement at fairs was very much a matter of secondary importance, as the fair was a major trading occasion. Fairs were often held on days of religious observation and their venue would have been the north side of the churchyard, if there was no other site available in the area. The function of a fair was to provide, under charter, the opportunity for the buying and selling of goods; booths were set up in the churchyard, where farmers and merchants brought their wares, where people foregathered not only to buy and to sell, but also to meet and to exchange ideas and to carry on all manner of business. The subsidiary needs of buyers and sellers were also met of course by the various booths, which catered for eating and drinking and for the amusement of their customers. Until the eighteenth century, when the state of the roads began to improve and canals began to prosper, local communities were very isolated and hence had to become self-sufficient. Periodic fairs were invaluable in helping to procure this self-sufficiency. In addition these fairs were places where strangers were allowed to sell their wares. Free trade was the hallmark of medieval fairs. To this end very often a large wooden hand or a stuffed outsized glove was displayed in a public place, often on a church, to give the necessary assurance that outsiders would for once be welcome. The hand in fact continued to be displayed many years after there was any need for this assurance to be given. Indeed in Chester a large glove was suspended on the walls of St. Peter's church every July and October for fourteen days before the fairs and for their duration, right up until the late 1860's, while elsewhere in the same county, in a chapel in the country church of St. Oswald in Lower Peover, not far from

Knutsford, can still be seen nailed to a wall a wooden hand, which may once have hung outside the church to indicate to all and sundry that the church gave its blessing to the holding of a fair in the churchyard.

DISSERTH

On the north side of the churchyard, where today goats graze, two hundred years ago parishioners made merry and not only on the day of the patronal feast. The same Shropshire lawyer whose description of the goings-on has already been quoted, on his way to Disserth caught up with a man leading a horse, which was drawing a sledge, bearing a cask of ale, also bound for the celebrations. When the lawyer arrived, he had to make his way through a crowded lane to get to the churchyard, which was thronged with people, dancing to a fiddler, who was sitting on a grave. The farm opposite the churchyard gate was until 1897 a public house, which played a central part in the festivities. The thirteenth century church, which stands in a large circular churchyard, suggesting a very ancient site, fortunately escaped the attention of restorers in the nineteenth century with the result that the interior is just as it was in the seventeenth century, with high-backed box pews, which bear the names and addresses of their seventeenth century occupants. In 1872, when the living fell vacant, Kilvert's name was put forward but alas for posterity the diarist heard nothing.

ABEREDW

The porch of this Radnorshire village church, which
lies above the Wye Valley, south of Builth, has double
tiers of stone seats where lawyers and merchants and
musicians at different times followed their respective
callings. Where now stand the graves in front of the
porch, in former times the village games were played.
The porch is flanked by two immense yew trees
between which, according to the local record, no
fewer than sixty couples were on special occasions
known to dance, while the walls of the tower will
have resounded to the noise of fives' balls, well into
the nineteenth century.

A Shropshire lawyer visited Aberedw in 1744 and
wrote an account of the local feasting on the patronal
day. He noted that the tops of the graves were used as
tables to hold the refreshments. The villagers danced
under the trees but "the quality danced in an erection
made of twigs and branches."

Until the passage of the Education Act in 1870 the
children of Aberedw attended a school which was held
in the tower of the church.

63

LLANBISTER

St. Cynllo's church stands high above the Radnorshire village; today's church, mostly built in the thirteenth century, was preceded by a Norman building in which Giraldus Cambrensis spent a night when trying to whip up enthusiasm in the area for the Third Crusade. Inside the church a musician's gallery, which was put up in 1716 for the use of the village band to accompany the service, bears the initials of the churchwardens, who will have had to organise many a church ale to pay for the purchase of the instruments. One of the monuments in the church is to the memory of a devoted nineteenth century vicar, who held the living for forty-nine years. One day, while riding his horse round the parish, he heard the sound of hymn-singing coming from a farmhouse; he investigated and found a Methodist service in progress, which so impressed him that in his will he left money for the building of a Methodist chapel. He was as good as his word; he died in 1838, the date-stone on the Methodist chapel is 1839.

This same vicar, David Lloyd, becoming concerned at the increasing attention being paid to eating and drinking in the churchyard on the annual patronal feast day in July, prayed for the intervention of a thunderstorm to sober up the miscreants. In the middle 1820s his prayers were answered when a terrifying storm coincided with the ending of the morning service, which had the effect, at least on that one occasion, of putting a stop to the usual fun and games in the churchyard!

6. GAMES IN THE CHURCHYARD

There is little doubt that for a very long time the north side of the village churchyard was the village playground, where at different times and in different areas, wrestling, quoits, nine-pins, hammer throwing, marbles, football and fives all had their devoted adherents; the most popular of these games, to judge by the frequency of contemporary references, seems to have been fives. The pursuit of such activities in the churchyard in no way incurred the displeasure of priests, because there are records showing that priests either participated themselves or actively encouraged such goings-on in churchyards. It is known, for instance, that in the Vale of Clwyd, in N. Wales, the vicar acted as scorer in games of fives, while Parson Woodforde mentioned in his diary on 22nd June 1764 that his "guests plaid at Fives in the churchyard this evening and I lost there at betting 0.1.6." However with the upsurge of Puritanism in the sixteenth century, the public attitude had changed somewhat for a time, the change of outlook being reflected in the mounting opposition to the unsuccessful attempt in 1617 by James I (and again in 1633 by his son, Charles I) to legitimize certain Sunday amusements in churchyards. Nevertheless churchyard games continued and in some parts, and more often in the Marches and in Wales, lingered well into the nineteenth century.

The popularity of fives would be hard to account for were it not for the fact that the buttressed north walls of churches and sometimes the towers were found to be ideal, ready-made courts. Indeed so great was its attraction in Wales and in the Marches that arrangements had to be made for the accommodation of spectators. There are references in churchwardens' accounts in the seventeenth and early eighteenth centuries to the spending of money on amenities for those who wanted to watch. Sunday afternoons seem to have been the favourite time for fives, but at Clocaenog in Clwyd the game was played by enthusiasts on Sunday morning before service. At Llandefalle in Powys, a few miles north-east of Brecon, there were until recently wooden shutters on the windows on the north side to protect the glass from fives' balls; a recent examination revealed worm-eaten parts of the shutters lying in the long grass under the north windows, with pieces of iron still attached to them, while iron hinges and iron stays are still firmly in position on the wall.

At Disserth in Powys in 1774 the same visitor, whose comments on the parish wake have already been quoted, also described ball games going on in the churchyard. "The church" he said "is a strong building, and pretty large, against the tiles of which were a dozen lusty young fellows playing at tennis and as many against the steeple (? tower) playing at fives . . .", while at Llanfair Discoed, in Gwent, by the middle of the eighteenth century future events were beginning to cast their ominous shadows over those who played ball games on Sunday. In the church porch may be read the following inscription.

Whoever hear on Sunday
Will Practis Playing at Ball
it May Be before Monday
The Devil Will Have you All.

The Methodist Revival was near at hand.

65

Over the border in Herefordshire there is considerable evidence that fives was popular; at two isolated hamlets high up in the Golden Valley at Llanveynoe and at Craswall churchwardens' accounts made frequent mention of money having to be spent on the repair of tiles and windows rendered necessary by the playing of ball games in the churchyard. The Royal Commission on Historical Monuments in its 1931 report said of Craswall "In the churchyard and running north from the chancel is a rectangular sinking in the ground with a flat floor. It is said to have been a fives court." Others have interpreted this as a cock-fighting arena. Certainly running around the north walls, both at Craswell and at Llanveynoe, there are wide stone ledges, which a local historian in the nineteenth century referred to as "stone seats for those who wanted to watch games in the churchyard."

Elsewhere in the Golden Valley, a few miles south-east of Craswall is the tiny hamlet of Newton St. Margarets against the north wall of whose church fives were frequently played. As at Llandefalle some of the iron hinges that carried the protective shutters over the window in the north chancel are still in place, and earlier in this century a horizontal red line was still visible in the plaster, above which the ball had to be aimed. Both at Newton St. Margarets and at Craswall stone slabs have been clamped securely to the north wall in the area where the game was played, prompting the thought that they might have served as score-boards.

Two further references to fives must suffice. At Bradford-on-Avon, in Wiltshire, according to a mid-nineteenth century report, "the tower shows unmistakable evidence of having been used for the balls of the players." Westwards in Cheshire, in the busy old market town of Nantwich, whose parish church is one of the architectural treasures of the county, the playing of fives was specifically forbidden in the churchyard as late as in 1776.

Of all the entertainments that went on in the north side of the churchyard none strikes a more discordant note to modern ears than cockfighting, which through the centuries until quite recent times was extremely popular with most sections of society. Originally introduced into Britain by the Romans, in Tudor times the sport was taken up by royalty; Henry VIII had a royal cockpit built and in his reign cockfighting became known as the "royal diversion." In the seventeenth century James I was an enthusiast, as was his grandson, Charles II. Trevelyan comments. "In later Stuart times the cock-fight was the most popular sport of all, on which all classes staked their money even more than upon horse racing." Cockfighting mains were held regularly in the seventeenth century in churchyards both in England and in Wales; there are even cases on record of cocks fighting in the naves of churches. In some parts no wake or festival was complete without this particular diversion until finally Parliament put an end to the disgraceful business in 1849.

From early on in the middle ages until the end of the nineteenth century in some places churchyard dancing of various kinds stayed popular; it was a regular occurrence on all special occasions, of which there were a great many, such as wedding feasts, church ales, patronal feasts and fairs. There were in addition ritual dances, such as those performed by the morris men. John Aubrey in the seventeenth century wrote. ''in Herefordshire and in parts of the Marches of Wales the tabor and pipe were exceedingly common. The peasants danced to them in the churchyard on Holy days and on Holy Day Eves.'' On the west wall of Aberedw church in Powys are hung two flutes, which were played in the church in the nineteenth century, and in all probability in the church porch also, because there is a local tradition that the musicians played there to accompnay those who danced outside between two enormous yew trees. This custom of dancing in the churchyard died hardest in Wales, which seems to have been a pleasure-loving country before the coming of Methodism. According to an ancient source *Malkin's* ''SCENERY AND ANTIQUITIES OF S.WALES'' ''the custom of dancing in the churchyard at their feasts and revels is universal in Radnorshire and very common in other parts of the Principality. Indeed this solemn abode is rendered a kind of circus for every sport and exercise.'' Methodism and other similar dissenting movements gained great momentum in the Principality in the eighteenth century. Just how great the need was for some change can be seen from the following account, written in Anglesey in 1799. ''The common people delighted in nothing except empty sport and carnal pleasures, playing with dice and cards, dancing and singing with the harp, playing football, tennis, mock-trials and hostages and many other sinful sports too numerous to be mentioned. They used the Sunday like a market day to gratify every wicked whim and passion; old and young, with no-one to persuade or prevent them in their ungodly course. They flocked in crowds to the parish churches on Sunday morning; not to listen to the Word of god but to devise and relate foolish anecdotes and to entice each other to drink and the wash-brew house of the devil's market, and to arrange places of meeting to decide upon the sports to be engaged in after the evening service. The lads and young men by the hundreds kicking the football all in their pants and shirts and belabouring each other more like dogs fighting for a bone than men bearing the name of Christian. The old men acting as spectators, encouraging and urging on every man his party; sticks in hand, they shouted and swore in a manner which made them look hideous. The women in scores contended and yelled at the tops of their voices; in their excitement and wild rage they would cast off their shawls, their hats and caps, more formidable in aspect than hags.''

Another unruly pastime which marginally had to do with churchyards was inter-village football. In Dyfed there was an annual mass game of football between Llandysul and Llanwenog. Any number of participants was permitted, the goals being the porches of the respective parish churches. Again in Wales, but further north in Powys a similar football match took place once a year on Christmas day between Glascwm and Betws Disserth, the pitch being the four miles of intervening countryside. Glascwm, which also at one time boasted a race-course, is today quiet and peaceful and eminently respectable, while all life has now gone from Betws Disserth whose church is no longer in use, not even as a goal!

The Methodist revival followed. There

can be no doubt that the success of these religious movements led to a decline in drunkenness and debauchery, the adoption of more serious attitudes to life and in general to higher standards of morality and conduct, but out with the evil habits went much that had previously brought seemingly innocent pleasure into the harsh lives of the poor.

By way of postscript another widely-observed churchyard custom, worth a passing mention, is the custom known as embracing or clipping the church. The children of a village assembled in the churchyard, joined hands and proceeded to move ever nearer the church. The time of year chosen for this unexplained custom varied from district to district; instances are on record of it being observed anytime from Shrove Tuesday to the middle of September. Sometimes a hymn was sung, occasionally a priest preached a sermon to the children from the porch of the church, but generally it was purely a secular affair. The ritual in Shropshire was honoured well into the nineteenth century both at Ellesmere and at Wellington. At the latter place a band of boys gathered in the town, equipped with tin trumpets, which they blew lustily, as they hurried towards the churchyard. There they joined hands and noisily clipped the church. In both towns the custom, which always took place on Shrove Tuesday, was an integral part of the general merry-making that preceded the solemn onset of Lent.

GLASCWM

In a remote and very beautiful valley in a wild part of
Radnorshire is the clas church of Glascwm, which is
dedicated to St. David and is traditionally believed to
have been founded by him. Built on a hill and circled
by yews, this sixth century site was probably
originally chosen for its previous religious association
with earlier times, in all probability with the Bronze
Age. The porch in former times used to act as one of
the goals in the Christmas Day inter-village football
match, referred to in the text.
For a description of some aspects of life in Glascwm in
the nineteenth century the reader is directed to
Kilvert's Diary, whose author visited the vicar one
May morning in 1871.

ST. MARY'S CHURCH, CRASWALL

This twelfth century Herefordshire church is situated
high up in the Golden Valley, under Hay Bluff, on the
eastern side of the Black Mountains. The large
churchyard seems to have had more secular than
religious significance as there are no signs of graves.
The illustrations show a stone seat running along the
south and east walls of the church, where spectators
were believed to sit while watching the various
pastimes that went on in the churchyard, of which the
best-known were fives and cock-fighting. The actual
site of the cock-pit has been presumed to have been in
the depression in the ground on the north side. Fifty
years ago a local resident remembered his father
telling him that his father had witnessed a cock-fight
there, while he himself had as a young man often
played fives against the wall of the church.

7. THE MEASUREMENT OF TIME

In Saxon days and throughout most of the Middle Ages there was a shortage of clocks; admittedly monasteries and abbeys were equipped with them, a special official, the sub-sacrist, being responsible for their maintenance. Cathedrals and many large town churches also possessed the luxury of clocks; among the earliest ones in cathedrals were those at Canterbury (1292), St. Albans (1326) and Wells (1390). Nevertheless village churches were for the most part without them. Every countryman of an earlier age than ours not only got up in the morning when the sun rose and went to bed at sunset but also relied on the sun to tell him the time. The church was the very centre of his restricted world and hence the earliest sun-dials were scratched on churches.

Furthermore life in medieval England was organised on such local lines and communication with other areas was so inadequate and unreliable that there was no such thing as universal time for all parts of the country. Even in the rare village where the church had a clock, it had at regular intervals to be corrected by the local sun-dial. From early Saxon times to the middle of the nineteenth century, when the opening-up of the country by the railway system made the acceptance of Greenwich Mean Time inevitable, sun-dials clearly played a very important role in the life of the community. In the twelve hundred years that elapsed between the making of the earliest known Saxon sun-dial and the early years of Victoria's reign, when sun-dials were finally abandoned, there were three different types of dials, which roughly corresponded with the pre-Norman period, the years from the Norman Conquest to the middle of the sixteenth century, and the post-Reformation years.

The Saxons divided the hours of daylight into four parts, which they called tides, 6 a.m. to 9 a.m., 9 a.m. to noon, noon to 3 p.m., and 3 p.m. to sunset. Their sun-dials are known as tide dials and the basic divisions corresponded with the times of the celebration of mass. The simplest Saxon dial consisted of a stone slab set in a south wall with a long horizontal line engraved on it to represent dawn and sunset. At right angles to it is the noon division and between dawn and noon and between noon and sunset are lines cut at 45° to mark very roughly 9 a.m. and 3 p.m. respectively. At the point of intersection of all the divisions, i.e. at noon, there was a hole in the stone into which an iron marker was inserted, known as a gnomon. This gnomon, of which unfortunately no specimen has survived, cast the shadow which told the time; its actual positioning was very important. Its shadow should have fallen on the noon line exactly at noon on Midsummer Day. Usually the intermediate lines between dawn and sunset, marked at 9 a.m., noon and at 3 p.m. were crossed by a short engraved line, thus forming a cross. Surviving Saxon tide dials in churchyards are rare, but specimens may still be seen at Bishopstone in Sussex, at Great Edstone, at Old Byland and Kirkdale in north Yorkshire and at Daglingworth in Gloucestershire.

The earliest known Saxon dial is at Bewcastle, where, unlike the others, it is engraved not on the church but on a cross in the churchyard. Bewcastle, situated in that remote part of Cumbria that lies north of Hadrian's Wall, has on the south side of the churchyard a most remarkable cross, which is thought to date from the year 670. This famous cross, which is now unfortunately only an obelisk, the cross having been removed some centuries ago, is elaborately carved on all four sides, with the sun dial on its south face standing about nine feet above the ground. This dial shows the day divided into twelve parts, but it is quite possible that some of the intermediate lines may have been added in after years. Only the lines marking 9 a.m., noon and 3 p.m. are crossed.

At Bishopstone in Sussex, not far inland from the coast at Seaford, is an ancient church, whose justified boast is that the most modern work there is Norman; of Saxon work, nothing is more impressive than a sundial engraved over the porch of the south door. Inscribed on it is the name Eadric. Further west, in Gloucestershire, north-west of Cirencester, there is another Saxon tide dial in the village church of Daglingworth, which contains a wealth of Saxon and Norman craftsmanship. The dial is almost typical but has one intermediate line of division between dawn and 9 a.m.

In north Yorkshire, high up above Sutton Bank, in the Hambleton Hills, lies the ancient and attractive market town of Helmsley, which has within an hour's drive from it three churches that possess Saxon tide dials, Old Byland, Great Edstone and the incomparable Kirkdale. The village of Old Byland is about four miles north-west of Helmsley, past the splendid abbey at Rievaulx; the church is mostly twelfth century, its Saxon predecessor having been savaged by the Normans. The Saxon dial has in the course of the years been shamefully treated, its very survival in the circumstances being fortunate and indeed fortuitous. Originally, according to records, the dial had been carved on a huge slab of stone, which had been inscribed Sumerlidan Hurscal Me Fecit. Sumerlidan clearly made the dial and he may have been a 'house carl'. The porch was rebuilt in the eighteenth century when the damage seems to have been done. The two end pieces of the slab that bore the inscription are now missing but the vital middle piece on which the dial was engraved survives on the east wall of the porch, where it acts as a quoin, having been inserted upside down. There is a very large hole for a gnomon and the divisions are at two hourly intervals.

About eight miles east of Helmsley and just over a mile south of the road to Pickering, is the compact village of Great Edstone, whose Saxon church still bears a tide dial above the south door. The slab on which the dial is engraved is four feet long and one foot eight inches deep. The mason's name above the dial is quite legible, Lothan, but most of the letters on the slab to the left of the dial, though visible, defy explanation. The three lines between dawn and noon and between noon and sunset suggest one and a half hour divisions.

Last and best of the north Yorkshire tide dials is over the south door of St. Gregory's Minster at Kirkdale, a church in a hidden valley under Ryedale, about seven miles east of Helmsley not far from the little market town of Kirkby Moorside. That the dial is still in such a wonderful state of preservation is due partly to the fact that a porch was built over the door in the twelfth century, (thus making the dial inoperative) and partly because at some later date it was covered with plaster; it was indeed the removal of this protective covering in 1771 that led to the discovery of the existence of the dial. The dial, which occupies the middle section of a slab of stone seven feet in length, is divided like the one at Great Edstone into eight parts; the divisions at 9 a.m., noon and at 3 p.m. are crossed. On the first dividing line, at 7.30 a.m. is a different sort of cross, which may well mark the time of the first service of the day. Above the dial are words which have been translated as "This is day's Sun marker at every time," and underneath is engraved "Haworth me wrought and Brand priests." Both ends of the slab, between which is the dial, contain sufficiently specific historical details to enable historians to attribute the carving of the dial to the year 1055, when a new Saxon church was built at Kirkdale to replace one destroyed in a Danish raid. In addition to these Saxon dials, there is another of equal antiquity and importance but seeing that it is to be found in the churchyard of Clynnog Fawr in Gwynedd it must be termed pre-Norman rather than Saxon! It stands south of St. Beuno's great church, and is carved on an upright pillar stone.

In Norman and later medieval times sun dials, though basically similar to the Saxon pattern, often had the full circle. They were generally subdivided into twelve sections and admitted of considerable regional variations in style. What is puzzling about medieval scratch dials, or mass dials as they are frequently called, is the lack of uniformity in their distribution. Although the need to know the time must have been equally keenly felt by everyone in all parts of the country in the Middle Ages, (it is known that trading times for markets were rigorously enforced) the fact remains that there are areas where scratch dials today are very scarce, while in other district, such as south Gloucestershire, there are a great many still to be seen, there being more than a dozen churches with scratch dials within a ten mile radius of Cirencester. Special mention is made of the following churches in that region because between them they possess more than thirty such dials. They are Ampney Crucis, Ampney St. Mary, Ampney St. Peter, Coln St. Aldwyns, Coln Rogers, Coln St. Denis, Eastleach Martin, Eastleach Turville, Quenington and Yanworth.

The puzzle of uneven distribution may be partly explained by erosion down the centuries; certainly some types of building stone have weathered very badly and on many church walls it needs very close scrutiny indeed to detect even vestigial traces of medieval scratchings. Again many medieval churches may have been insecurely built. It has to be remembered too that there was great prosperity in the Middle Ages in the area around Cirencester, where some of the vast profits made from the wool trade were devoted to the building of magnificent churches. At any rate many churches had to be restored or rebuilt altogether from Tudor times down to the end of the nineteenth century. Their restorers seem not always to have known about vertical scratch dials on the walls, as several walls in Cheshire and Herefordshire will bear witness, their scratch dials having been so built around in the restoration that the dials became no longer able to tell the correct time. At Tarvin, not far from Chester, there are three scratch dials together on the south wall of this twelfth century church, all immediately underneath a window, which must have been put in position after the dials were engraved, because just above the dials the stones, on which the gnomons would have been inserted, are missing, presumably discarded when the window was built. In addition the post-medieval south porch juts out so far that the dials would have been in shadow most of the day. Further north in the county, at Grappenhall, just south of the Mersey, near Warrington, the stone on which a dial was scratched now faces north-west, indicating that the Tudors, who rebuilt that part of the church in the sixteenth century, were either in ignorance of its purpose or deliberately chose to ignore it. There are two other medieval scratch dials in Cheshire that are clearly recognisable; one is to be found on the south porch of St. Mary's church in Cheadle, having managed to survive several restorations of the porch, while the other is on a buttress on the south wall of the church at St. James', Audlem, in the south of the county. For many years it remained undiscovered, hidden under a protective covering of ivy, which has now been replaced by the preferable protection of a glass-covered box.

In the south-west of Herefordshire in the massive church at Garway there is, adjoining the chancel, a thirteenth century chapel, whose east wall was rebuilt by the Tudors. In strengthening the corner with a buttress they made use of a scratch dial, putting it in upside down. There are however two excellent scratch dials in the county, the first being at Kingstone, a village six miles south-west of Hereford. The dial here is unusual because it is carved on the tympanum of a window on the south wall. Though the only divisions marked with lines are at three-hourly intervals, there are hourly marks in the perimeter of the stone.

The other Herefordshire dial, a splendid and quite remarkable one, is on the chapel of Dinmore Manor, a private house, in the words of Pevsner," far away from any village, up a small, secluded, well-wooded valley." The access road is a turning off the A49 between Leominster and Hereford. Engraved on the south wall, probably in the fourteenth century, it has fifteen lines radiating from the central gnomon; these lines are marked in Roman numerals, two of which are incorrectly placed, as the XI should be interchanged with the IX. There is evidence of another dial on the west buttress of the south door, of which the gnomon hole and six incised divisions are still visible.

Whether it was because scratch dials were no longer thought reliable, either through erosion, bad siting or later building coming between them and the sun, or for some other reason to do perhaps with the brave new world ushered in by the sixteenth century with its Renaissance and its Reformation, in Elizabeth's reign there were new sun dials, which were to be quite different from the old ones. They were no longer scratched on vertical walls of churches; instead horizontal plates, often of metal, marking the hours, were fixed on the top of stone shafts in the churchyard on the south side of the church, mounted on the remains of medieval crosses. Most dials erected between Elizabeth's and Victoria's reigns corresponded to this pattern, though a few

continued to be put up, generally on
brackets, on the south walls of churches.

DAGLINGWORTH

The village church at Daglingworth, a few miles north
of Cirencester, is unusually rich in Saxon remains,
one of which is the tide-dial over the south door,
which was to become unusable when a porch was
later added; by way of compensation later on in the
Middle Ages a scratch dial was carved on the south
wall of the porch. In the foreground is what remains of
a medieval preaching cross and between this and the
church porch are several plain table tombs.

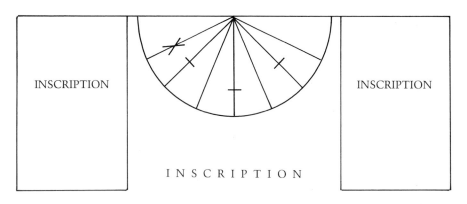

INSCRIPTION

INSCRIPTION

I N S C R I P T I O N

SAXON DIAL AT KIRKDALE

The inscriptions either side of the Kirkdale dial have
been thus deciphered "Orm Gamal's son bought St.
Gregory's Minster when it was all broken down and
fallen and let it be made anew from the ground to
Christ and St. Gregory, in Edward's days, the King
and in Tosti's days, the Earl."
The different type of cross on the line in the first tide
between dawn and 9 a.m. probably indicated the time
of a service.

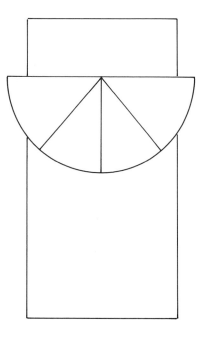

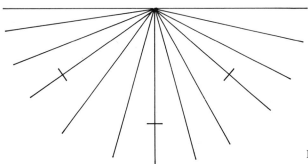

SAXON DIAL ON BEWCASTLE CROSS

Inscribed on the cross are the words "First year of the
King of the realm, Ecgfrith." This gives the
approximate date of 670 for Bewcastle and makes it
the earliest known Saxon tide-dial.

PRE-NORMAN DIAL AT CLYNNOG FAWR

The church at Clynnog Fawr, near which this dial is
carved on a separate pillar stone, is dedicated to St.
Beuno, whose dislike of all things Saxon caused him
in the seventh century to move from his home in
eastern Wales to the Saxon-free security of the Lleyn
Peninsula. This dial, put up of course several
centuries after Beuno's time, is unlikely to owe
anything to Saxon influence but clearly the Celts and
the Saxons, at least in the reckoning of time, had
something in common!

SCRATCH DIAL AT DINMORE MANOR

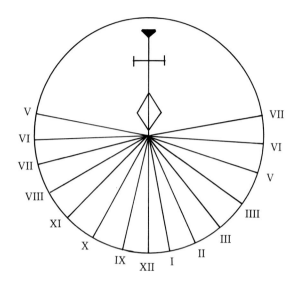

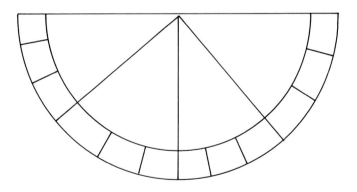

SCRATCH DIAL AT KINGSTONE

8. CHURCHYARD BURIALS

It was the same Pope Gregory who had despatched Augustine to these shores who first advised burying the dead in churchyards rather than in cemeteries. Christians attending service would then see the graves of the departed as they approached the church and would be, it was hoped, the more likely to remember the dead in their prayers. Despite this spiritual authority for burial in churchyards, a great deal of superstition often accompanied funerals. From somewhere came the notion that the devil, whose non-existence in the eyes of the church never seems to have stopped a great many Christians from believing in the reality of his existence, could claim the first body buried in a newly-consecrated churchyard. There are even occasional accounts in early records of the first Christian burial in a churchyard being preceded by the unofficial interment of a dog. Another frequently recurring idea concerned the posthumous duties of the most recently buried corpse; he or she, many believed, became the 'watcher' in the churchyard until relieved of that irksome duty by the next funeral. This office of watcher was considered unpleasant and a duty to be avoided wherever possible; so widespread indeed was the belief in its truth that occasions have been recorded where in the event of two funerals taking place on the same day unseemly haste was shown by the funeral parties in an attempt to outwit each other in the timing of the committal. To complete this little chronicle of superstition, when in later years the burial space in a churchyard was nearing exhaustion, it was thought unlucky to be the last person interred, presumably because eternal vigilance might be the fate of the deceased. To escape this awful destiny it was sometimes agreed to bury the body upside down, as this was believed efficacious in cancelling out the posthumous duty.

Bodies were normally buried on their backs with their heads to the west so that their eyes were looking towards the east; this established mode of Christian burial probably had its origin in pagan sun worship. Instances have been given of north-south burials but where investigation has followed, it has appeared that the burial had been either of a non-Christian or of a Christian who had fallen foul of the church authorities. Traces of sun worship continued to manifest themselves in funeral rites for many years; wherever possible, things had to be done clockwise, or, as devotees preferred to say, 'sunways'; for instance, in some villages the procession insisted on going to the church clockwise. Anti-clockwise was regarded as very unlucky and was known as "going the back way". In one case the villagers went even further by carrying the corpse three times round the churchyard cross clockwise; the disapproving vicar preached against the pagan practice to no avail until in desperation he destroyed the cross, being careful to hide the fragments.

The lych-gate, which was usually on the south side of the churchyard, was the setting for the first part of the funeral service in the Middle Ages; lych means body and the lych-gate was always roofed to protect the priest and the funeral party, who placed the shrouded body on the seat, where the priest took charge and performed the opening obsequies. The corpse was then placed on the parish bier and pushed along the path to the south door of the church. The second part of the service took place in the porch before the final solemnities were observed in the chancel, prior to a return to the south side of the churchyard for the committal.

As late as the seventeenth century superstitions concerning corpses seem still to have been rife among ordinary people, if John Aubrey's diaries are to be believed. Writing before the Civil War he remembered hearing old people talk about putting a penny into the mouths of corpses, to be given to St. Peter; he also called to mind that when he was a boy 'it was a common fashion for the women to get a tooth out of a skull in the churchyard, which they wore as a preservation against the toothache.''

It was not until the second half of the seventeenth century that coffins began to be used for the burial of ordinary people; shrouds remained in common use until the eighteenth century, when coffins became fashionable. In some areas a parish coffin, generally of a flimsy quality, was available for carrying the body to the grave. Towards the end of the seventeenth century the priest had an extra duty to discharge at the lych-gate because in 1678 Parliament, in an attempt to give a much-needed impetus to the wool trade, which was then in decline, ordered that all bodies should be buried in wool. Thus the priest had the additional task of making sure at the lychgate that the shroud was made of wool before it was placed on the bier or secured in the coffin. This act was repealed in 1814, but between 1678 and 1814 many references are to be found in church-wardens' accounts to the care taken to see that the law was carried out, the penalty for the infringement of which was £5. In general the entries are confined to the statement that so-and-so ''was buried in wool'' although an exception is to be noted in the records of Shocklach church in south-west Cheshire, where one Anne Povey was buried in March 1678. The entry reads ''neither wrapped nor wound in any shift, sheet or shroud or anything else but what was made of sheep's wool only.'' Occasionally an extra conscientious churchwarden thought it necessary to buy a register book for the entry of ''burials in woollen'', the usual price for which seems to have been about five shillings.

Throughout the Middle Ages, when those who had become outstanding in the life of the community were given burial and remembrance inside the churches, the ordinary man stayed outside in the churchyard, where uncoffined and anonymous corpses, wrapped in cloth, were deposited in the ground, one on top of another, until the level of the south side of the churchyard rose and the churchwardens were presented with a problem of overcrowding. In many places it is clear that the problem was left unsolved with results that are still apparent today in the high banks at the side of the paths that led to the south entrance of the church, as at St. Nicholas' church, Montgomery in Powys. It has been noted that Thomas Gray in his Elegy Written in a Country Churchyard was relying overmuch on poetic imagination when he wrote:

''Each in his narrow cell for ever laid,
The rude forefathers of the hamlet
   sleep.''

For, the usual solution to this problem of overcrowding was to erect a small charnel house to which what have been nicely referred to as "undecayed relics of mortality" were removed and stored in neat rows. Often too the charnel houses themselves became overcrowded and occasionally there are reports in churchwardens' accounts of bones being unceremoniously tipped into large pits, usually known as mortuary holes. This then was the general pattern of churchyard burials until well into the seventeenth century.

Before dealing with subsequent developments, a diversion must first be made to the unconsecrated north side of the churchyard, where throughout the Middle Ages and indeed much later still in some parts, the burials took place of people who had transgressed so badly in the eyes of the church authorities that burial in consecrated ground was quite unthinkable. Normally this fate was reserved for those who had taken their own lives or the lives of others. The parish register in the Cheshire town of Malpas recorded in 1667 the death of "H. Sarah Harrison, who hanged herself . . . she was buried on the backside of the church." This harsh attitude seems to have mellowed with the passage of the years but even so feeling against burial on the north side was very slow to evaporate, despite the pressing need to do so when space became scarce for further interment on the south side. Gilbert White, in a letter written in the 1780s, talked of the unpopularity that still attended north side burials. He said:—"All wish to be buried on the south side, which has become such a mass of mortality that no person can be there interred without disturbing or displacing the bones of his ancestors."

Back to the seventeenth century, which was a time of marked social and economic change; there was a considerable rise in living standards for very many people, despite the unhappy social consequences that had followed the dissolution of the monasteries in the previous century. As this increased prosperity slowly spread down the social scale it gave rise to a new middle class which came to occupy the middle ground between the haves, who in the seventeenth century tended to have more, and the have-nots, whose poverty thereafter was slightly less debilitating. The effects of these changes can be seen clearly at work in country church and churchyard, where the most affluent members of the new middle class were sometimes able in death to acquire monumental equality with squires and landowners and prelates of the church. Keeping up with the Jones' may be a modern phrase but it expresses an idea which was certainly prevalent in the seventeenth century, where lesser but more numerous members of the new class were quick to seek, if not parity with their more prosperous contemporaries, at least a parallel social advance in death. For they not only had their names inscribed at their places of burial but the very shape and appearance of their newly-acquired gravestones bore a marked resemblance to the more splendid memorials seen inside the church. Things were beginning to look up for the ordinary man, even if his greater importance first became obvious only when he was dead. In life he would have noticed inside the church grave slabs and wall tablets and maybe solid table tombs.

When in the seventeenth century our forebears decided to extend the privilege of named burial to those buried in the churchyard, it was natural that they should try to copy the types of memorials with which they had all their lives been familiar in the church. The earliest named graves in the churchyard, dating from the late sixteenth or early seventeenth centuries, were either horizontal stone slabs like those set in the floor of the chancel or short thick mostly unadorned vertical slabs of stone in crude imitation of wall tablets. These vertical gravestones, usually on an east-west orientation, had the memorial slab at the west end, with the inscription carved on the east side of the stone, facing the grave and thus enjoying some protection from the ravages of the prevailing west wind. Later in the same century many headstones were higher and wider and thinner. It seems probable that these early gravestones, whether they were squat and vertical or thick and horizontal were made by local general masons, whereas the monuments inside the church were the work of specialised craftsmen. The trade of monumental mason probably dates from the early eighteenth century.

Contemporary with these vertical stones were horizontal slabs of stone called ledgers, which had for many years been a common sight in the chancels and transepts of churches, where they had been suitably inscribed with the names and achievements of the deceased. The translation of this type of grave to the churchyard involved the sinking of a heavy slab, several inches thick, into the earth. Frequently the consequence was that it sank further than was intended and speedily became covered by vegetation. Many must have been obliterated in this way until the lesson was learned and the slab was raised on low supports. Despite wind erosion on headstones and encroaching vegetation on ledgers, there can still be found a representative selection of these early churchyard memorials. In the north of Cheshire in the vast churchyard that surrounds the fine old church at Astbury it is still possible to read the inscriptions of more than fifty seventeenth century ledgers, while a few miles further north in the same county may be seen in the churchyard at Wilmslow a tombstone with the name clearly legible of a woman who was buried there in 1596.

Another type of tombstone appeared outdoors for the first time towards the end of the seventeenth century, namely the table tomb, a type that had first been erected inside churches in the thirteenth century. The seventeenth century specimens that remain are plain and substantial with sufficient room for later burials to be recorded and commemorated on the side and end panels. An excellent example may be found in the churchyard of a twelfth century church at Sarnesfield in Herefordshire, a few miles west of Leominster, where one, John Abel was buried in 1674. This old craftsman, who in his ninety seven years did much to provide his native county with splendid market halls, designed his own tomb, on the lid of which he had carved, along with his personal details and epitaph, the tools of his trade, his compasses, his set square and his foot rule --- truly a social record in stone. Such table tombs, erected as this one was near the south porch, were sometimes used as convenient tables for the distribution to the poor of various sorts of alms made available by charitable bequests. An unusually large number of such tombstones may be observed in the churchyard of the diarist, Kilvert's old church at Bredwardine, also in Herefordshire. In the eighteenth century table tombs in some places ceased to be plain and unadorned but began to carry much ornament and decoration. This development can most clearly be seen in the Cotswolds. So-called bale tombs, thought by some to indicate the wealth made from the production of wool, are particularly striking in appearance, as will be observed in the illustrations of a pair of such graves at Bibury and of a double-decker example in the peaceful churchyard of Shipton-under-Wychwood.

While most churchyard memorials were made of stone because supplies of the commodity were plentiful, in some parts where slate was quarried, a very durable alternative to stone was at hand. A few slate headstones date from the seventeenth century but slate did not pass into general use until the early years of the eighteenth century; by the middle of the following century many slate quarries had been worked out. In areas associated with iron-founding iron gravestones were very common. To this day many survive in Sussex but the greatest concentration of iron memorials is around Coalbrookdale in Shropshire, where the Industrial Revolution had begun.

From humble beginnings of ledgers and headstones later developments were comparatively slight; ledgers came more and more to be lifted off the ground and headstones were better proportioned and carved with more skill and sophistication. It has to be emphasised that, while developments in the design and decoration of ledgers and headstones were only of a minor nature, elsewhere in the churchyard there was a great burgeoning of craftsmanship. The years from the middle of the eighteenth to the middle of the nineteenth century constituted the golden age of achievement in churchyard memorials, the years when the stonemason's art derived great strength and inspiration from classical sources. In the southern part of the Marches in parts of Gwent, Powys and Herefordshire, an outstanding contribution in this field was made by a family of craftsmen, called Brute, of whom Aaron was the most distinguished. The plain table tombs of the early years yielded place to the richly ornamented and magnificently embellished chest tombs which can be seen at their very best in the Cotswolds, more particularly in the churchyard at Painswick, in Gloucestershire, where marvellous decorated horizontal tops stand next to pedestal tombs, set on square, circular or occasionally octagonal bases and sometimes surmounted by classical urns. Such memorials, though the glory of our churchyards, were not erected above the bodies of ordinary men but rather commemorated the affluent and famous, who in earlier centuries would have found lapidary remembrance inside the church. The storied urns and animated busts did not immortalize the remains of ordinary men, who continued to have erected above their graves raised ledgers or headstones or perhaps after 1850 gleaming white crosses.

Epitaphs constitute a specialised study which is not being attempted here; certain salient points about them are nevertheless worth noting. Up to the nineteenth century the commonest feature of memorial verses was concern with human mortality. 'As I am now, so will you be'' is a recurring theme. Interest in death was obsessive and the following inscription would have raised no contemporary eyebrows. It comes from a grave in the Cheshire churchyard of St. Michael's, Macclesfield. "Mary Broomfield. Dy'd 19th. Nov. 1788. Aged 80. The chief concern of her life for the latter years was to order and provide for her funeral. Her greatest pleasure was to think and talk about it. She lived many years on a Pension of 9d. a week and yet saved £5, which at her own request was laid out in her burial. Reader, think not this short history useless. Excuse what thou mayst think folly and by her example learn a lesson of the greatest wisdom—to be mindful of thy latter end."

In the eighteenth century there was little evidence of Christian beliefs on tombstones. The sudden widespread interest awakened in Europe's classical past served to combine with the traditional fear of Roman Catholicism to produce an attitude of apathy towards established religious ideas. In addition, the affairs of the Church of England were at a very low ebb at this time. The mood changed and by the beginning of the next century the advance of Methodism and the successes of the Sunday School movement together helped to add Christian sentiments to memorial inscriptions.

The chief interest of these inscriptions, Christian or pagan, to the social historian lies in the light they throw on contemporary life and problems. For example, painstaking research has shown that in those inscriptions that reveal the occupations of the deceased, no fewer than forty different trades and professions have been listed. This register, which covers the period from the restoration of the monarchy in 1660 to Victoria's golden jubilee, contains the following:—Actor, angler, auctioneer, barber, brewer, bell ringer, blacksmith, brickmaker, builder, carpenter, coachmaker, clockmaker, cricketer, doctor, exciseman, falconer, farmer, fencing master, gamekeeper, gardener, horse dealer, innkeeper, miller, musician, painter, parish clerk, poacher, prize fighter, railway engineer, ratcatcher, roadmaker, sailor, schoolmaster, servant, shepherd, shoemaker, soldier, stonemason and waggoner. Here is a rich tapestry indeed,—Everyman in his many different coats. Memorial inscriptions, taken in conjunction with churchwardens' accounts, provide excellent source material for the study of such social problems of yesterday as the size of families and infant mortality, although such enquiries are hardly likely to satisfy the curiosity of the observer, when confronted by the inscription on an iron chest tomb in the Shropshire churchyard of Madeley. The laconic message runs thus:—"Her warfare is accomplished."

MONTGOMERY

This view, taken from the path that leads to the south porch of St. Nicholas' church in Montgomery, clearly shows the consequences of the practice that prevailed before the seventeenth century of burying the dead on top of each other. Very often churchwardens tackled this problem of overcrowding by removing earlier burials to the charnel house but, where this was not done, as in Montgomery, the result was a dramatic change of levels in the churchyard.

ASTBURY

Situated in a rural area just south of Congleton, in north-east Cheshire, St. Mary's church is a truly magnificent edifice; apart from its porches previously commented upon, the enormous churchyard is of outstanding interest to the social historian. There is a very rare early fourteenth century canopied tomb, much eroded of course, and a wealth of ordinary gravestones both horizontal and vertical, dating from the seventeenth and eighteenth centuries. There are also many ancient yews and the base of a medieval preaching cross with the customary eighteenth century sundial mounted on its truncated shaft. The photograph shows the grave of a young blacksmith who died in the middle of the eighteenth century.

BIBURY

In this view of the south side of the churchyard at
Bibury, one of the most-visited villages in the
Cotswolds, attention is drawn to the two table tombs
near the porch as well as to the double bale tombs in
the foreground.

SHIPTON-UNDER-WYCHWOOD

There are many different types of table tombs in
Cotswold churches; the one shown here, in the
churchyard at Shipton-under-Wychwood, is unusual
in that it is a double-decker, one tomb with a bale top
having been erected over a flat table tomb. There are
two burials and two separate inscriptions.

9. THE STRANGE AFFAIR OF THE BODY SNATCHERS

In the second half of the eighteenth century the peace and tranquillity of our churchyards was suddenly and sensationally ruptured by the sinister activities of men who came to be known as the Body Snatchers or Resurrectionists. In 1745 barbers and surgeons agreed to go their separate ways; thereafter the training of surgeons became more thorough and more rigorous, involving the acquisition of some knowledge of human anatomy. Hence the need arose for bodies to be made available for dissection; this need was only partly met by the provisions of a law passed in 1752 which authorised the transfer of the bodies of executed murderers to London medical schools. The surgeons' further wants were to be supplied by means that were certainly unethical but unfortunately not illegal, since there was no specific law against the theft of corpses, though there could be a prosecution for trespass or for the theft of such incidentals as a ring on a corpse.

The first completely authentic instance of body snatching seems to have been the theft of the body of Mrs. Jane Sainsbury in 1777, when it was removed after interment in a burial ground near Gray's Inn in London. Mystery surrounds the disappearance of an earlier corpse, that of Laurence Sterne, the distinguished author of Tristan Shandy, who died in March 1768. He was buried in the churchyard of St. George's, Hanover Square in London, from which his body was removed four days later. Legend has it that a body snatcher sold the corpse to the Professor of Anatomy at Cambridge, who is alleged to have gathered around him a group of his friends to demonstrate to them his skill in dissection. There was some embarrassment when, according to report, one of the professor's friends, who happened also to have been a friend of the dead author, recognised the identity of the body. As there is apparently no reliable evidence to corroborate this story, explanation is still awaited for the disappearance of Sterne's body.

Not far away, in another part of London, and at about the same time, the needs of anatomists at St. Bartholomew's Hospital were being satisfied by body snatchers, who operated in the churchyard of St. Sepulchre. Contemporary opinion held that the villains stored their corpses in a hostelry nearby in anticipation of future profitable sales to the hospital. In an attempt to stop this particular source of supply, a watch house was built in 1791 in the churchyard from which to mount guard over new graves. These watch houses, or watch boxes, as they were called in some places, looked rather like sentry boxes, though some were rather more elaborate and were equipped against marauders. In various parts of the country other means were adopted to try to put a stop to the activities of the body snatchers. At Warburton, in north Cheshire, there is still a hole to be seen in an old oak door in the west tower, which, according to local tradition, watchers cut two hundred years ago to give themselves an unimpeded view of miscreants entering the churchyard.

Sometimes heavy boulders were rolled into place on newly-dug graves; in many a churchyard up and down the country boulders will still be pointed out. In the churchyard at Pannal, just south of Harrogate, is a medieval stone coffin of immense length known locally as the Resurrection Stone. It weighs over a ton and in the days of the body snatchers was hired out at a guinea for two weeks. When placed on top of a grave, it satisfactorily defeated all efforts to steal corpses. In some vulnerable areas bodies were occasionally buried in iron coffins, while iron was also sometimes used to make strong fences around graves. Such protective railings were known as mortsafes and were especially common in Edinburgh, where body snatchers acquired more notoriety than anywhere else. Sometimes spring guns were set by relatives after a funeral but the practice was discontinued when it proved unsuccessful. It was observed that the setting up of such a gun was frequently followed by the appearance in the churchyard of a woman in deep mourning who spared time from her grief to detach the wires of the gun!

According to an article published in the Lancet in 1896 the body snatchers obtained their bodies in the following way. "Several feet, 15 or 20, away from the head or foot of the grave, the resurrectionist would remove a square of turf, about 18 or 20 inches in diameter. This he would carefully put by and then commence to mine. Most pauper graves were of the same depth and, if the sepulcre was that of a person of importance, the depth of the grave could be pretty well estimated by the nature of the soil thrown up. Taking a five-foot grave, the coffin lid would be about four feet from the surface. A rough slanting tunnel, some 5 yards long, would therefore have to be constructed, so as to impinge exactly on the coffin head. This being at last struck (no very simple task)

the coffin was lugged up by hook to the surface, or preferably the end of the coffin was wrenched off with hooks while still in the shelter of the tunnel, and the scalp or feet of the corpse secured through the open end and the body pulled out, leaving the coffin almost intact and unmoved. The body once obtained, the narrow shaft was easily filled up and the sod of turf accurately replaced. The friends of the deceased, seeing that the earth over the grave was not disturbed, would flatter themselves that the body had escaped the resurrectionists, but they seldom noticed the neatly-placed square of turf, some feet away."

There was also published in 1896, a diary kept by the leader of a gang of 7 body snatchers who operated in London in the early years of the nineteenth century: the surviving entries in the diary covered the thirteen months from November 1811 to December 1812 in which time more than 500 bodies were dug up and sold to hospitals. The leader retired early, with sufficient money to build a large hotel in Margate while another member of the gang at his death left £6000, which was a considerable sum of money at that time. The legality of stealing bodies was tested in the courts in 1814 when three members of the gang just mentioned were caught in charge of a horse and cart, which contained 7 bodies. At their trial they were all acquitted. A more publicized trial took place at Lancaster Assizes in 1827, when a Warrington surgeon was charged, along with others of obtaining the body of a young woman from a Baptist churchyard near Warrington. The surgeon admitted paying £4 for the body, which was taken from its grave 3 days after burial. The case was referred to the Old Bailey in London, where the surgeon was fined £20, not for stealing the corpse, which was not a crime, but for having in his possession something which he knew to have been stolen. This did amount to a criminal offence.

In the churchyard at Mottram in north-east Cheshire is a memorial stone to a 15 year old boy who was buried there in October 1827. The subsequent removal of the body provoked the following inscription.

"Though once beneath the ground his
    corpse was laid,
For use of surgeons it was then
    convey'd;
Vain was the scheme to hide the
    impious theft,
The body taken, shroud and coffin left.
To wretches who pursue this
    barbarous trade
Your carcases in time may be convey'd
Like his, to some unfeeling surgeon's
    room
Nor can they justly meet a better
    doom."

In that same year 1827 the best known events of this grim and grisly business came to a head in Edinburgh, where an Irish labourer, William Hare kept a lodging-house to which another Irishman, William Burke came to lodge. Later that same year another lodger in the house, a pensioned sailor died and the two Irishmen joined forces and sold the body for £7-10 shillings to Dr. Robert Knox, a famous Edinburgh anatomist. The prospect of future riches beckoned to the two villains, who thereafter abandoned themselves to procuring the deaths of other poor men, who were enticed to this and to other lodging-houses, where, suitably plied with drink, they were to meet their deaths by suffocation. Burke and Hare in this way obtained 15 bodies which they succeeded in selling for sums ranging from £8 to £14. The law eventually caught up with them in 1829; after Hare saved his skin by turning King's Evidence, Burke was executed. Robert Louis Stevenson's famous story "The Body Snatcher" is believed to have been based on the life of the infamous Burke.

Thomas Hood, in a poem called Mary's Ghost, dealt with this macabre subject.

"The body snatchers, they have come,
And made a snatch at me;
'Tis very hard-them kind of men
Won't let a body be.
The cock it crows-I must be gone
My William, we must part;
But I'll be yours in death although
Sir Astley has my heart."

This Sir Astley Cooper was a famous surgeon of his day who must have been singled out for this reference because he had been trained in Edinburgh; his reputation seems not to have suffered through the poet's gibe, as he became President of the College of Surgeons and Vice-President of the Royal Society before his death in 1841.

The day of the body snatcher was nearing its close. In 1830 two of their number were caught after stealing two newly buried bodies from the churchyard in Alderley, in Cheshire. At the subsequent trial it was discovered that the charges that could be brought against them were trespassing and stealing a wedding ring from one of the bodies. Public anger which had been mounting for some time, now demanded action. Two years later, in 1832, the same parliament that had passed the First Reform Bill, passed the Anatomy Act, which satisfactorily brought the scandal to an end. Thereafter not only were anatomy schools required to be licensed but body snatching was specifically recognised as a crime to be punished by fine and imprisonment. Peace at last returned to the churchyard. Sadly, by way of postscript it has to be added that in the eighties of the twentieth century another kind of peace has descended upon the churchyard that surrounds a famous old parish church in the north of England, the peace conferred by surreptitious glue-sniffing!

Part III

1. CHURCH FESTIVALS AND SOCIAL CUSTOMS

In this last section, it seems appropriate to refer back once again to the initial problems which Christian missionaries in these islands had to contend with in early days. One of the hardest to overcome was the devotion of the pre-Christians here to their pagan customs, many of which probably had their roots in a prehistoric culture. Pope Gregory in his celebrated letter to Mellitus asked him, according to Bede, to counsel Augustine on his behalf to treat the pagans gently, "for there is no doubt that it is impossible to efface everything at once from their obdurate minds." The advice was heeded and although the early Christian fathers set their hearts against some pagan practices, such as the bringing of mistletoe into church, they did, by allowing many customs to continue, set the seal of authority upon many hitherto non-Christian practices. Even so progress was slow; just how slow the process of acceptance of the new religion proved to be can be judged from a later reference in Bede to the circumspection shown in the seventh century by Redwald, King of the East Saxons, who maintained two altars in the same building, one for Christian worship, the other for sacrifice to pagan gods. "In the infancy of the Christian religion" wrote John Aubrey in the seventeenth century "it was expedient to plough with the heifer of the Gentiles."

A thousand years later and the situation in this respect seems to have changed very little; George Herbert, himself a man of the Marches, writing in the early years of the seventeenth century, had this to say. "The country parson is a lover of old customs, if they be good and harmless, and the rather because country people are much addicted to them, so that to favour them therein is to win their hearts and to oppose them therein is to deject them. If there be any ill in a custom that may be severed from the good, he pares the apple and gives them the clean to feed on."

*   *   *   *

Nowhere in the Christian calendar is the marriage of the old and the new, the pagan and the Christian more obvious or indeed more felicitous than in the celebration of Easter. Early Christians in their wisdom saw to it that the remembrance of Christ's resurrection should coincide with the pagan celebration of the Spring solstice, just as the celebration of Christ's birthday was arranged on the 25th December to coincide with the annual welcome accorded by pagans to the Winter solstice. At Easter, in addition, Christians and pagans shared a common interest in eggs. The church with its insistence on self-denial in Lent had forbidden the eating of eggs, on Shrove Tuesday the last of the eggs being used up in the making of pancakes; hence it was only natural that eggs would be very welcome indeed on Easter Sunday, when the ban on their consumption expired. This obvious Christian interest in eggs at Easter fitted in very neatly with the ancient pagan belief, which was widespread in many

91

early societies, that the earth itself was not only egg-shaped, but had been actually hatched from an egg. Hence in the Spring the egg was the symbol of rebirth to Christians and pagans alike. Christian children have for a long time now been brought up to expect a chocolate egg at Easter, while, more particularly in Cheshire, for very many years children have been encouraged to go round the farms to ask for "an egg for Easter." In the central Cheshire village of Great Budworth, children still make their annual visits to the farms and on Easter Sunday afternoons they take their eggs to a special service in the parish church where the eggs are blessed before being sent to local hospitals.

On Palm Sunday in the Middle Ages there was a great procession through the north door of the church right round the churchyard and back into the church through the south door, commemorating Christ's triumphant entry into Jerusalem; today Palm Sunday still announces the approach of Easter to Christians and the arrival of Spring to everyone in these islands, Christian or otherwise. Customs associated with this day either grew up during the centuries or were taken over by the church and tailored to their own requirements. Thus in many parts the churches were decorated on Palm Sunday either with willow or yew and the graves in the churchyards were made gay with spring flowers. In some counties, much attention was paid to this decoration of graves, a custom which in Wales was usually observed the previous day.

Three Herefordshire villages, not far from each other, Kings Caple, Sellack and Hentland have for about four hundred years had their own special Palm Sunday

ceremonial. Thanks to a sixteenth century legacy from Lady Scudamore, cakes and ale were provided for the morning service on Easter Day in the three village churches; these were distributed at the end of the service by the churchwardens. The cakes, which were round and flat, had stamped on them the Lamb and Flag, the emblem of St. John the Baptist, to whom the church of Kings Caple, the largest of the three churches, was dedicated. Today no beer is served but after the service the vicar hands round a so-called Pax cake to every member of the congregation, saying as he does so "God and good neighbourhood", as tradition requires. In former times there was an additional ceremony as those who had quarrelled with each other in the previous year met in the church porch, shared a cake and made their peace.

Before coming to customs to do with Easter Sunday itself, mention first should be made of one local custom, which appears to have been peculiar to Shropshire, the custom on Maundy Thursday of going to the nearest holy well and dipping one's head in it. A great many wells that the church had made holy had in former generations been held in veneration by our pagan forebears and this attention paid to wells on Maundy Thursday may well be yet another example of Pope Gregory's advice being taken!

In some southern parts of the Marches the decorating of graves took place not on Palm Sunday but on Easter Eve. Kilvert, in a long entry in his diary on Easter Saturday 1870 described the custom in Clyro. ". . . At eleven I went to the school to see if the children were gathering flowers and found they were out in the fields and woods, collecting moss, leaving the primroses to be gathered later in the day . . .'' In the early evening he went into the churchyard and commented thus. ''Now the customary beautiful Easter Eve idyll had fairly begun and people kept arriving from all parts with flowers to dress the graves. Children were coming from the town and from neighbouring villages with baskets of flowers and knives to cut holes in the turf . . . more and more people kept coming into the churchyard as they finished their day's work. The sun went down in glory behind the dingle, but still the work of love went on through the twilight and into the dusk until the moon rose full and splendid . . . the flowers most used were primroses, daffodils, currant, laurel and box.'' Next evening Kilvert, having preached at the Easter Day services, noted in his diary the smart appearance of the congregation. ''On Easter Day all the young people come out in something new and bright as butterflies. It is almost a part of their religion to wear something new on this day.'' Further north, in Shropshire, as indeed in many more places too, great attention was paid to wearing new clothes on Easter Day, when Nature too was putting on a fresh coat of green.

At one time in several different parts of the country traditional feasting of a sort went on in church on Easter Day. One such tradition had been observed in the church at Berrington, south-east of Shrewsbury. Here a row was brewing in 1639, when the bishop saw fit to interfere with a time-honoured usage. According to the local record ''there hath been time out of mind an ancient custom used within the parish of Berrington that the parson of the said parish hath yearly on Easter Day

feasted all the parishioners and landholders with a love-feast, the solemnization of which was ever yet performed in the church.'' This usage the bishop would no longer allow; the local squire disagreed and an English compromise resulted. The parishioners were allowed to continue the enjoyment of their feast and the parson would be obliged to continue to pay for it, but it could no longer be held in the church nor could it take place on Easter Sunday. The custom eventually died out there in 1713.

Of all the customs and ceremonies connected with the celebration of Easter none surpasses in interest the rather bizarre happenings of Easter Monday and Tuesday when certainly in Cheshire and Shropshire, as well as in other counties further to the east, what was termed Heaving or Lifting took place. To begin with, Easter Monday was a public holiday and therefore a time for relaxation, which could and often did descend into horse-play. Two ideas lay behind this strange custom, one religious, the need to remember the resurrection of Christ, the other social, the necessity of doing everything possible to ensure the success of the next season's crops. The basic practice was for young men on Easter Monday to waylay young women and to lift them up, that is to say for two of their number first to hold each other's wrists to form a make-shift chair; when their victim was safely on their chair, she was as a rule compelled to pay a forfeit before being restored to the ground. On the next day, Easter Tuesday the roles were reversed and men were required by custom to submit to what may be surmised to have been gentler treatment than that accorded to the young women the previous day. Public opinion in the long run saw to it that the custom was dropped, but there are a number of surviving accounts of the ceremony before hooliganism made the practice no longer socially acceptable.

In 1798 a visitor to Shrewsbury was having his breakfast in the Talbot hotel (today Woolworths stands on the site!) on Easter Tuesday, when he was made aware of the local custom. He wrote:—"I was surprised by the entrance of all the female servants of the house, handing in an armchair, lined with white and decorated with ribbons and flowers of different colours. I asked them what they wanted, the answer was that they came to heave me; it was the custom of the place on that morning and they hoped I would take a seat in their chair. It was impossible not to comply with a request very modestly made by a set of nymphs in their best apparel and several of them under twenty. I wished to see all the ceremony and seated myself accordingly. The group then lifted me from the ground, turned the chair about and I had the felicity of a salute from each."

Forty Easters later another such incident was recorded, also in Shrewsbury. According to one of the participants, "I recollect a few years ago accompanying Joseph Palmer Esq., to Acton Reynald on Easter Tuesday and being very much amused. My friend had a particular aversion to the custom of lifting; he had escaped from a posse of his own tenants' wives and daughters in Coleham, Shrewsbury, and fought through a host of resolute females assembled in the Castle Foregate, but at Acton Reynald he could neither fight nor run away. Soon after our arrival a chair was introduced into the room in which we were sitting, handsomely adorned with ribbons and flowers, followed by all the female members of the family, who with smiles of cheerful modesty requested the honour of lifting us; the highly distinguished owner of the mansion, Sir Andrew Corbet, Bart., had previously honoured the group with his compliance, then who with the smallest degree of good nature could afterwards refuse? Mr. Palmer was subdued; we were each three times raised above our level to the innocent diversion of all parties."

*   *   *   *

To our pagan forebears May Day was the happiest and most important day in the whole year; the winter was at last over, the sun was gaining strength and was riding higher in the heavens, the crops were beginning to grow. The first of May was set apart for welcoming this wholly beneficent change. Men and women, while grateful for the improvement in their fortunes, looked forward in anxious speculation to the coming season, the fertility of their fields and their beasts being uppermost in their minds. Hence fertility rites came to be associated with the general rejoicing on May Day, the maypole being first and foremost a phallic symbol. The Romans in their turn had grafted their own ceremonials on to the existing merry-making of that day. On the last four days of April and the first day of May Early Romans, themselves still living close to the soil, made merry in honour of their floral goddess, Flora.

Christians, faced with the familiar problem of having to deal with time-honoured pagan practices, for a time tried to christianise existing May Day practices. Quite early on however they seem to have come to the conclusion that the social pressures at work on May Day were too great to be diverted into any obviously religious channels. In consequence Christians set apart the three days that preceded Ascension Day, itself being observed on the fortieth day after Easter, for celebrations that it was hoped would succeed in wooing pagans away from their own May Day excesses. Easter, of course, is a movable feast and its celebration had to be indeed early in the year if the days of Rogation were to be anywhere near the day that the Christian church so much distrusted. The underlying purpose of Rogationtide was for the church authorities to bless the crops; it was the second of the four outstandingly important Christian rites that deal with the needs of a rural society. The ploughs were blessed on the first Monday after the Epiphany, the crops were blessed at Rogation, at Lammas on the first Sunday in August the first fruits were offered in church and at Harvest came the festival of thanksgiving.

There was however in addition an important secular side to these days of Rogation; it was the beating of the bounds, when parishioners, led by the priest and the choir, walked round the parish. In days, when maps and records were few, this annual marking out of the boundaries of the parish was very important indeed. Customs in connection with it varied considerably in different parts of the country, but in all parts, it seems the choir sang psalms and the priest read passages of the Bible. Periodically the procession came to a necessary halt and then the priest at a suitable vantage point, generally at a tree,

would read from the Gospel. Such trees were known as Gospel Trees; many of them are still to be found marked on Ordnance Survey maps. A number of such trees can still be seen in Herefordshire. In some areas the perambulation did not take place until Ascension Day, as was the general practice in Shropshire.

In Shrewsbury the beating of the bounds was energetically accomplished every Ascension Day up to about 1850. There were five parishes in the town, hence the annual demarcation exercise gave plenty of scope to those with energy to work off or old scores to settle. Such parochial processions bore little relationship to the ceremonies of earlier times, when not only the boundaries were made clear but God's blessing on the crops was invoked. On the morning of Ascension Day, in all five parishes, bands of schoolboys, led by the churchwardens, the beadles and sextons set forth from their respective parish churches. Contemporary accounts speak of the hideous noise that came from the boys' trumpets. All carried long wands, generously decorated with bunches of spring flowers, known as Bannering poles. Indeed the Ascension Day rite throughout Shropshire was called Bannering. Generous bystanders provided food and drink for the walkers at their numerous stopping-places. Occasionally two bands met each other where boundaries converged and a great deal of violence resulted. Violent clashes of this sort, frequently made worse by too liberal an intake of the liquid refreshment provided, probably hastened the end of a social custom that had outlived its usefulness.

There was a similar beating of the bounds in Wenlock on Ascension Day but it died out before the end of the eighteenth century; at Wem, north of Shrewsbury, along with the beating of the bounds went a fair, called the Rig Fair, where girls were hired for the year as domestic servants. In the south of the county, at Ludlow, the bannering took place on Rogation Wednesday but here apparently standards of behaviour were higher. Boys from the various schools, led by their priest, went in procession from the parish church, stopping at the site of a former cross, where the lesson of the previous Sunday was read, before going on to the Weeping Cross, where prayers were said. After the boundaries had been confirmed, the procession broke up at the Guildhall for refreshment, plum buns being the traditional and popular reward the boys received for their efforts.

From Cheshire, where the beating of the bounds was a general feature of Rogationtide ceremonies, churchwardens' accounts speak of very considerable sums being spent on refreshments. Walking, of course, is thirsty work, but the impression is gained that a good time was had by all! Between 1600 and 1750 there are references in churchwardens' accounts to the costs involved in the perambulations at Bidston, Bruera, Shocklach, Tarporley, Wallasey and Weaverham.

*   *   *   *

For once the Christian church had no earlier pagan ritual to contend with; the field was clear for the Christians. Whitsunday was Pentecost, the fiftieth day after Easter, when the Holy Spirit descended upon the disciples; in the course of time it became one of the three great baptismal occasions, the white clothes traditionally required for the baptismal service giving its name to the day, White Sunday. Despite the absence of pagan antecedents, gradually non-religious observances attached themselves to the celebration of Whitsun. Many a churchwarden found himself superintending the erection of that most pagan of symbols, a maypole, while Morris dancers frequently performed on the north side of the churchyard, and on Whit Monday the greatest church ale of the whole year would have filled the churchyard with noise and merriment, if the sun were shining, and the very nave of the church itself, if the weather drove the parishioners indoors.

In the Middle Ages, particularly, the religious side of Whitsun was stressed, predominating over the secular celebrations. In some churches following the morning service on Whit Sunday a dove was solemnly freed from its temporary captivity under the roof and allowed to flutter to freedom through the nave to the open south door. A general practice in the Marches was to decorate the church with the leaves of trees; in Shropshire the birch was particularly favoured. Boughs of it were fastened into holes on the tops of the pews. At two churches in Shrewsbury, St. Mary's and St. Chad's, and at Hordley, near Oswestry, the practice continued well into the middle of the nineteenth century. In Herefordshire too the birch was much used for this purpose on Whit Sunday, though at Kington local tradition demanded yew instead of birch for the decoration of the church. The foliage of both birch and yew was, of course, brilliantly green at this time of year.

Kilvert, writing in his diary in 1871,

referred to a report of Whitsun customs he had read in a local paper, which he summarized thus. "The hallowing of churches at the stroke of twelve, mysterious visits to the graves of friends, scattering on the graves the last blooms of May, letting loose a white pigeon in honour of the Holy Dove, maidens dressed in white, waiting in silence in church chancels as if in expectation of a celestial descent." Whitsuntide seems to have been similarly celebrated in Cheshire, with one or two local additions. At Farndon, in the south-west of the county, near the Welsh border, the graves in the churchyard were covered with rushes on which flowers were scattered, while in the church stems of asparagus were fixed in the holes on top of the pews to which bunches of flowers were attached. A contemporary witness commented. "All the body of the church was one mass of waving green plumes." Further north in Chester itself Whitsuntide saw the annual performance of mystery plays, in which twenty-five guilds cooperated to depict on a two-tiered cart the whole story from the creation of the world to the Last Judgment.

*   *   *   *

Long before the Christian church designated the first two days of November as saints' days, their pagan predecessors had held them in special veneration. At the end of October and the beginning of November winter was approaching fast; it was a time of change which was marked in a number of different ways. A feast was held to do honour to the dead and festive rites accompanied the piling-up of bonfires, when the air above was believed to be thick with ghosts and witches. The Christian church had to struggle hard with these earlier, deeply-ingrained ceremonies but win she did eventually so that today we have All Hallow E'en, followed by All Saints' Day and All Souls' Day. The struggle was keenly fought and long after the victory had been assured some of the earlier customs were seen to have survived remarkably well under a thin veneer of religious respectability.

On the night before All Saints' Day fires came to be sanctioned by the church, though the reason for them was a practical one, quite unconnected with any primitive ritual. As churchyards became evermore dangerously overcrowded with uncoffined bodies, bones had from time to time to be removed to a charnel house which was usually to be found in the churchyard. On All Hallow E'en the charnel houses that had in turn become uncomfortably full were emptied and the bones consumed in a fire, in order to make room in the charnel houses for a new supply of bones from the churchyard. These fires were much appreciated, especially by those whose ancestors would have celebrated the onset of winter with similar fires, which had in the old days been lit to drive off evil spirits and to encourage the dying sun to maintain its waning strength.

There is an interesting carry-over from pagan to Christian times in the association of All Hallow E'en with divination and prophecy. Many thought that on that special night (and in some parts on Midsummer Eve too) the very future might be looked into. Reference has already been made in the chapter on church porches to Kilvert's assertion that some parishioners on All Hallow E'en used to sit in the church porch at midnight and hear from within the church the names being called out of those who were destined to die in the following year; all this was little more than a century ago.

All Saints' Day on the first of November was called into being to mark the conversion of the pagan Pantheon in Rome into a Christian church. Over the years Christians have tended to commemorate on that day those saints for whom no special days of remembrance had been set apart; in addition, the dead, too, were remembered then in a practical way, because the custom had grown up to collect money for the saying of masses for them on the following day, All Souls' Day. To summarize, on November the first Christians thought of the dead and on November the second went to church to pray for the souls of those who were believed still to be enduring the pains of Purgatory.

Throughout the country much thought was given at that time of the year to the dead; Christians, particularly in the Middle Ages, prayed for their souls, while those less religiously inclined dwelt upon ghosts and the like, who were supposed to be unusually active just then. The completely non-religious customs associated with All Hallow E'en merged into the church-going and the praying of the two following days. A word much in use on both days was Souling; in order to prepare for the necessary praying for the souls of the dead, souling involved parties of people going round the parishes to collect money for the masses, but in the course of time the custom changed into something very different, as the emphasis passed from the requests for money to the begging for food and drink. In Shropshire souling parties tended to go out on November the first, while in Cheshire it was often on the following day. Whichever day was favoured, the custom varied very little in the two counties; children, and occasionally adults, went round the parish, calling on houses, as at Christmas, and singing a song, the words of which were basically the same everywhere, though with local variations.

The doggerel ran like this.
"Soul! Soul! for a soul cake
I pray, good missus, a soul cake
An apple, a pear, a plum or a cherry
Any good thing to make us merry."

It has to be borne in mind that the soul-cakers after all were the same children who a day or two before had made merry in an anything but religious way on All Hallow E'en. In the Market Drayton area of north Shropshire the above lines were immediately followed by:—

"One for Peter, two for Paul,
Three for Him, who made us all."

Despite this belated religious reference, souling, as it developed, owed more to Mammon than to God. Nevertheless it was a time of generosity; certainly in Shropshire there are a number of local records that comment on the munificence of house-wives, who were in the habit of filling baskets, and even clothes baskets, with cakes and fruit, which they left at their gates for children, and not exclusively children, to help themselves. The last woman in the Shropshire village of Pulverbatch to provide soul-cakes died in 1853, at the age of 101; it was said of her, according to the local record, that on her hundredth birthday she arrayed herself in her wedding dress of yellow satin and went to church in the company of her friends and neighbours and there received holy communion.

In Cheshire the records of the village of Over, which lies in the middle of the county between Northwich and Nantwich, show the continuity of souling from the middle ages to nearly the end of the nineteenth century, but whereas in former times the men and women of the parish put on their best black clothes and went round the village, ringing hand-bells and pleading with their fellows to think of those in Purgatory and to pray for their release from their torment, by the time that the custom fell into disuse a hundred years ago boys merely blackened their faces before knocking on the doors of houses in the village and singing the following song.

"You gentlemen of England, pray you
    now draw near
To these few lines and you shall hear
Sweet melody of music all on this
    evening clear
For we come a-souling for apples and
    strong beer."

At Malpas, in south-west Cheshire, a hundred years ago the rector wrote a letter to a local paper in Chester in which he made this complaint. "I have just heard three middle-aged men with a concertina singing a really sweet chaunt with words to the effect that all they they souled for was cakes and strong beer."

An additional attachment to souling in Cheshire was the performance of a play after the visits to the village houses for cake and beer; the actors were called Soul-cakers and the play which was normally performed on All Souls' Day was confined to the villages around Northwich. Early in this century most villages in this neighbourhood had their own variation of a very ancient ritual in which the common ingredients were the restoration of a dead man to life, the appearance of a man dressed up as a woman and towards the end of the play the hilarious entrance of a hobby horse. Today the tradition of the mummers' play is still kept alive in villages in the Comberbatch area.

2. THE CHANGING SCENE

Henry VIIIth's breach with Rome, followed as it was twenty years later by the religious settlement of Elizabeth, which together comprised the Reformation in Britain, completed the break with the Middle Ages. For reasons social as well as religious the unity of life in the parish was fractured; change, probably inevitable, had set in. The century after the initial quarrel with Rome witnessed a great increase in religious intolerance towards Roman Catholics who were either slow to change or quite unwilling to accept the ways of the new church. In this tense atmosphere another threat to the authority of the newly established Church of England grew apace, the threat of those who dissented, the Puritans. Late sixteenth century and early seventeenth century local records clearly register these new attitudes and new problems that followed in the wake of the Reformation.

Half a century after the villagers of England had had to withstand the stresses and strains that accompanied a religious schism, they were faced by the hatred and suspicions that were engendered by the Gunpowder Plot and after less than half a century again they had to endure the much fiercer and more terrible challenge of civil war in the 1640s. There were no clearcut geographical lines separating those who supported the King from those who backed Parliament. Many a village was actively involved in the fighting and many a village church and churchyard provided the battlefield. Churches were strong points, held against besieging troops, their thick walls and stout doors three hundred and more years later still bearing the visible wounds of war. Again and again, churches were called into use either to provide quarters for the soldiery or places of confinement for prisoners, who showed their resentment of their situation by the damage they succeeded in doing to their places of captivity.

Churches and churchyards suffered serious losses in the civil wars and in the days of the commonwealth that followed the defeat of the royal cause. All the pent-up fury felt by the Puritans towards the established church, which in their eyes still treasured too many emblems of their Roman Catholic past, found expression, in the years that separated the death of Charles I from the accession of his son, in the breaking of those churchyard crosses that had survived, the defacing of statues and the destruction of priceless medieval glass. Of this unhappy period Trevelyan wrote. "The Puritans had made men 'eat religion with their bread' till the taste of it sickened them." Excess begets excess, the Puritan back-lash of the 1650s gave place to the anti-Puritan repression of the 1660s and 1670s. By the end of the century, however, the storm seems to have blown itself out and in the reigns of William III and Anne something of a religious revival began that was to last about fifty years. It was in Anne's reign that Addison reported on life in the village church. "It is certain", he wrote, "that country people would soon degenerate into a kind of savages and barbarians, were there not such frequent returns of a stated time in which the whole village meet together with their best faces and in their cleanliest habits, to converse with one another . . . hear their duties explained to them and join together in adoration of the Supreme Being."

The accession of George III in 1760

coincided with a period of stagnation in the Church of England, at least at the local level. It is true that in the course of the eighteenth century country parsons had risen in the world, but as their standing in society had improved, both socially and economically, so the gap had tended to widen between the pulpit and the pew. At about the same time William Cowper visited many country churches in England in the company of a clergyman friend; his comments on what he observed on this tour he later gave to a cousin. In this letter he wrote. ". . . The ruinous condition of some of these edifices gave me great offence; and I could not help wishing that the honest vicar, instead of indulging his genius for improvements . . . by converting half an acre of his glebe land into a bowling green, would have applied part of his income to the more laudable purpose of sheltering his parishoners from the weather, during their attendance on divine service . . . It is no uncommon thing to see the parsonage house well thatched . . . while the church perhaps has scarce any other roof than the ivy that grows over it . . . The noise of owls, bats and magpies makes the principal church music in many of these ancient edifices; and the walls, like a large map, seem to be portioned out into capes, seas and promontories by the various colours by which the damps have stained them . . . in other churches I have observed, nothing unseemly or ruinous is to be found except in the clergyman and in the appendages of his person . . . but, if I was concerned to see several distressed pastors, as well as many of our country churches in a tottering condition, I was more offended with the indecency of worship in others. I could wish that the clergy would inform their congregations that there is no occasion to scream themselves hoarse in making the responses . . . that he who bawls the loudest may nevertheless be the wickedest fellow in the parish, while a word or two of instruction might not be thrown away upon the younger part of the congregation, to teach them that making posies in summer time and cracking nuts in autumn, is no part of the religious ceremony . . ."

Perhaps the criticism, which is sometimes levelled at the way the Victorians carried out the restoration of country churches in the next century, should be tempered by the recollection that no matter what the architectural losses sustained by some of the churches so restored, at least these churches became weather-proof and once again fit and proper places of worship.

*   *   *   *

All this is yesterday. The play is over, the actors have departed, but some of the properties remain—a broken cross, a clump of yew trees, a medieval scratch dial on a southern wall, a leaning lichen-covered tombstone. Those things proclaim the reality of the past in many a country churchyard but it is no longer a continuing reality. It has become a history book, but a book that is still worth the reading, especially as the print is fading fast.

Bibliography

Bede	Ecclesiastical History of the English Nation
H. S. Bennett	The Pastons and their England
F. Burgess	English Churchyard Memorials
G. G. Coulton	Medieval Panorama
J. C. Cox and C. B. Ford	Parish churches of England
O. L. Dick (ed.)	Aubrey's Brief Lives
J. Finberg	Exploring Villages
Giraldus Cambrensis	Journey Through Wales
C. Hole	A Dictionary of British Folk Customs
W. G. Hoskins	Fieldwork in Local History
D. M. Stenton	English Society in the Early Middle Ages
J. Strutt	The Sports and Pastimes of the People of England
W. E. Tate	The Parish Chest
G. M. Trevelyan	English Social History

Index of Places